# Financial Analyst's Indispensable Pocket Guide

**Ram Ramesh, CFA**

**McGraw-Hill**

New York   San Francisco   Washington, D.C.   Auckland   Bogotá
Caracas   Lisbon   London   Madrid   Mexico City   Milan
Montreal   New Delhi   San Juan   Singapore
Sydney   Tokyo   Toronto

**Library of Congress Cataloging-in-Publication Data**
Ramesh, Ram.
    Financial analyst's indispensable pocket guide / Ram Ramesh.
      p. cm.
    ISBN 0-07-136156-1
    1. Finance, Personal—Handbooks, manuals, etc.  2. Investment
analysis—Handbooks, manuals, etc.  3. Portfolio management—
Handbooks, manuals, etc.  I. Title.

HG179 .R3144 2000
332—dc21                                00-055396

# McGraw-Hill

*A Division of The McGraw·Hill Companies*

    8   9   0    DSH/DSH    0   1   0   9   8

ISBN 0-07-136156-1

*The sponsoring editor for this book was Kelli Christiansen, the editing super-
visor was Maureen B. Walker, and the production supervisor was Charles
Annis. It was set in Times Ten by North Market Street Graphics.*

McGraw-Hill books are available at special quantity discounts to use as premiums and sales promotions, or for use in corporate training programs. For
more information, please write to the Director of Special Sales, Professional
Publishing, McGraw-Hill, Two Penn Plaza, New York, NY 10121-2298. Or
contact your local bookstore.

This publication is designed to provide accurate and authoritative information
in regard to the subject matter covered. It is sold with the understanding that
neither the author nor the publisher is engaged in rendering legal, accounting,
or other professional service. If legal advice or other expert assistance is
required, the services of a competent professional person should be sought.
—*From a Declaration of Principles jointly adopted by a Committee of the
American Bar Association and a Committee of Publishers.*

The profession of financial analysis and portfolio management has seen significant change and growth since the days of Graham and Dodd. Newer and more complex concepts have been developed with more research every year.

However, it is virtually impossible for any professional to maintain, at his or her fingertips, all the details of these concepts and terms, let alone deploy them at work in a meaningful and effective manner. I realized this when I completed my CFA® (Chartered Financial Analyst) program and attained the coveted three letters. The vast number of concepts and terms learned during the program were quickly receding to the back of my mind soon after the dreaded exams were over. I realized the truth of the dictum, "If you don't use it, you lose it."

This pocket guide is a response to that need, which I recognized as widely felt not only by CFA charter holders but also by financial analysts and portfolio managers everywhere. It is designed to serve as a single source—a compendium of all the essential concepts, terms, and definitions that are invaluable to practicing financial analysts and portfolio managers in the industry.

The pocket guide is structured under 10 topic sections, with related terms and concepts organized within each section. These topic areas are arranged alphabetically as:

1. Behavioral Finance

2. Derivatives

3. Economics

4. Equities

5. Ethics

6. Financial Statement Analysis

7. Fixed Income

8. Portfolio Management

9. Quantitative Techniques

10. Real Estate

Whenever necessary, cross-references are provided within each section as well as across sections.

In creating this pocket guide, I relied on numerous publications that cover the subject matter, and these reference materials are listed in the bibliography. However, if there are any errors they are entirely on my account.

Ram Ramesh

# CONTENTS

# SECTION 1

# Behavioral Finance

## Agency Friction

The apparent conflict between the objectives of the money manager (the agent) and the plan sponsor (the principal) leads to agency friction. Agents manage the fund with short-term objectives with a view to ensure that the portfolio looks good; principals need their portfolios to be managed on a long-term basis. The result is friction between the agents and their principals.

(*See also* Myopic Loss Aversion.)

## Asset Segregation

Investors tend to separate their assets and evaluate them individually rather than in an integrated manner. This approach runs counter to rational economic theory, which holds that investors evaluate choices by viewing the combined outcome of their investments.

(*See also* Mental Accounting.)

## Biased Expectations

Analysts tend to be overconfident in their prediction of uncertain outcomes. This leads to biased and inaccurate expectations of the future.

A typical illustration of biased expectations occurs when investors have experienced embarrassing losses in their investments. Rather than being rational and cut their losses by selling, investors tend to hold on. This response contradicts the theory of rational economic behavior, which holds that investors' beliefs and actions are objective, rational, and unbiased.

(*See also* Rational Expectations Hypothesis: Section 3.)

## Decision Framing

An investor's decision can be largely influenced by how the decision is "framed." In other words, the decision will depend on the way the problem is posed. A problem posed in a negative way may yield a very different decision from the same problem posed in a positive way.

For example, when a stock is down, stockbrokers may frame the situation in such a way that the stock can be recommended as a "value buy" as opposed to a "sell." The framing will influence investors' choices.

## Equity Premium Puzzle

Equities have historically outperformed bonds and T-bills by about 7 percent. Such a large equity premium suggests that investors are highly risk-averse; otherwise they would not demand such high compensation for the additional risk of holding stocks over bonds. Yet investors are not known to be highly risk-averse. The puzzle is explained by two behavioral finance concepts. (*See also* Mental Accounting; Myopic Loss Aversion.)

## Loss Aversion

According to the widely accepted theory of rational economic behavior, investors are risk-averse. However, observed behavior demonstrates that investors are "loss-averse"—that is, they are averse to losses, not to risk per se.

More precisely, investors are risk-seeking in the domain of losses and risk-averse in the domain of gains. When investors are faced with a probable loss, they seek to take more risk in the hope of making a gain; when investors are faced with probable gains, they seek to avoid risk in the hope of minimizing potential loss.

## Mental Accounting

Investors tend to segregate their investments into separate mental accounts, such as dividend accounts and capital gains accounts. Thus, they do not view their investments in a consolidated way; instead, they consider the outcomes from each "mental account" separately. This leads to investor preferences for, say, dividends over capital gains and to a failure to consider total return.

## Myopic Loss Aversion

Investors who evaluate their portfolio performance frequently, with a disproportionately high sensitivity to losses relative to gains, are said to exhibit myopic loss aversion. This behavior is explained by the hypothesis that investors are risk-seeking in the domain of gains and risk-averse in the domain of losses. (*See* Loss Aversion.)

For example, Kathleen is saving for her retirement, some 25 years away. Her time horizon is long and therefore her risk tolerance should be high. However, with her ready access to technology, Kathleen evaluates her portfolio almost every day. She also tends to be highly upset when her portfolio is down but not as exhilarated when the portfolio is doing well.

Pension plan managers typically exhibit myopic loss aversion because of the inherent conflict between the short-time horizon in which their performance is evaluated and the long-term horizon of the pension plan liabilities.

## Reference Dependence

Investment decisions are largely based on the investor's reference point. Investment options are evaluated according to gains and losses relative to some reference point. These reference points are susceptible to manipulation, depending on the investor's preference.

Suppose that Kim buys the stock of ABC Tech Company at $10. Within weeks its price shoots up to $40—an increase of 400 percent. When the stock later falls to $30, Kim feels a loss of $10 rather than a gain of $20. The price of $40 has become a new reference point.

## Representativeness Heuristics

Investors tend to overestimate the probability that a "good" stock is a stock of a "good" company. Thus, investors tend to overpay for stocks from good companies and are unwilling to consider stocks of "bad" companies, even though such investments may actually have the potential for greater total return.

# SECTION 2

# Derivatives

## American Option

*See* Options.

## Arbitrage Opportunity

Arbitrage is a chance to make riskless profit with virtually no investment.

For instance, the stock of ABC Company is listed on the New York Stock Exchange (NYSE) as well as the London Stock Exchange (LSE). At a given point in time the stock is trading at $18 on the NYSE and at $16 on the LSE. An investor can make a riskless profit of $2 per share (ignoring transaction costs) by buying ABC stock on the LSE and selling it on the NYSE on the same day. This is known as arbitrage.

In an efficient market, arbitrage opportunities will be quickly eliminated. Rational investors will move in to take advantage of the opportunity and this will quickly close the gap. Any rational price for a financial instrument must eliminate the opportunity for arbitrage.

## Backwardation

The theory of normal backwardation holds that futures prices tend to increase over the life of the futures contract because of the general tendency of hedgers to be net short of a commodity. It is based on the belief that natural hedgers in the marketplace—say, coffee growers—wish to use futures to shed their risk. The coffee growers' primary aim is to ensure that they can get a guaranteed price at the time their coffee is ready for delivery. Hence, they will take a short position to deliver coffee and, in their eagerness to ensure a guaranteed price in the future, will sell at a futures price that is less than the expected spot price on delivery date.

Typically, backwardation occurs when the market is dominated by sellers of futures contracts. Figure 2-1 shows the patterns of futures prices in normal backwardation.

(*See also* Contango.)

## Basis

Basis is the spread between the spot and futures price of a security. It can be expressed as $S - F$, where $S$ is the spot price and $F$ is the futures price of a security.

## Figure 2–1   Backwardation

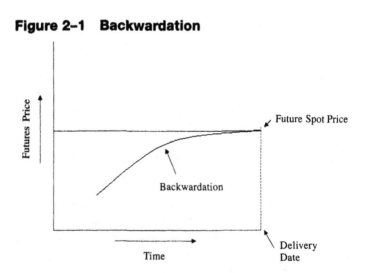

Owing to the theory of riskless arbitrage, the spot and the futures price converge on the settlement day. Thus, the basis is zero on the settlement day of the futures contract.

## Black-Scholes Option Pricing Model

Two renowned academicians, Fischer Black and Myron Scholes, developed a formula that can be used to value a call option. It uses the following factors in pricing the call option:

- Stock price
- Exercise price
- Risk-free interest rate
- Time to expiration
- Standard deviation of the stock return

**FORMULA**

The Black-Scholes pricing model can be represented by the following equation:

$$C = S\,N\,(d_1) - K\,e^{-rt}\,N\,(d_2)$$

where:

$C$ = Value of a call option

$S$ = Stock price

$N(d)$ = Value of the area under a normal curve from the extreme left tail to $(d)$

$K$ = Strike price of the call

$d_1 = [\ln\,(S/K) + (r + 0.5\,\sigma^2)t]/\sigma\sqrt{t}$

$d_2 = d_1 - \sigma\,\sqrt{t}$

$r$ = Risk-free rate (continuously compounded)

$t$ = Time to expiration measured in fractions of a year

$\sigma$ = Annual standard deviation of the stock return (volatility)

**ASSUMPTIONS**

The Black-Scholes pricing model is based on several assumptions:

- Returns for the security are normally distributed.
- The risk or variance on the underlying security is constant.
- Interest rates are constant for the period.
- There are no instantaneous price jumps in the security.
- No dividend or cash payments are received from the security during the period.
- There is no early exercise of the option on the security.

The Black-Scholes model is used to price options as well as to spot arbitrage opportunities in the securities market.

## Calendar Spread

Calendar spread is the spread between two futures price of different expiration dates.

It can be expressed as $F_{n1} - F_{n2}$, where $F_{n1}$ is the futures price for a contract expiring in day $n1$ and $F_{n2}$ is the futures price for a contract expiring in day $n2$.

## Call Swaption

*See* Swaptions.

## Cash-and-Carry Arbitrage

In a cash-and-carry arbitrage, a trader takes advantage of the differential between the prevailing interest rates and the implied repo rate in a futures contract. In other words, a cash-and-carry arbitrage opportunity exists when the futures contract is overpriced and/or market interest rates are lower than that implied by the futures price. The steps of a cash-and-carry arbitrage are as follows.

At time 0:

- Borrow funds for time $t$.
- Buy goods.
- Sell a futures contract to deliver the goods at time $t$.

At time *t:*

- Deliver the goods.
- Receive payment.
- Repay loan with interest.
- Pocket the difference.

(*See also* Covered Interest Rate Arbitrage; Implied Repo Rate; Reverse Cash-and-Carry Arbitrage.)

## Collar

A collar is a combination of a long (bought) put and a short (sold) call. The long put protects the downside while the short call finances the purchase of the put. A collar limits the owner's upside potential as well as downside risk.

## Contango

Contango, the opposite theory of *backwardation,* states that a futures price must exceed the expected future spot price. According to contango, hedgers are natural buyers of a commodity and desire to guarantee a firm price for the commodity in the future. Hence, they will be willing to pay a small premium above the expected futures price to guarantee the availability of the commodity and its price.

For instance, silver is an important ingredient for the film processing industry. Firms in this industry will wish to ensure the availability of silver at a fixed price when it is required at a future date. Therefore, they will bid a higher price than the expected futures spot price.

Typically, contango prevails when the market is dominated by buyers of futures contracts.

See Figure 2-2.

(*See also* Backwardation.)

## Contract Size

The number of futures contracts required to hedge a particular investment position is called the contract size. It can be calculated using one of many standard hedge ratio formulas. (*See* Hedge Ratio.)

## Figure 2–2   Contango

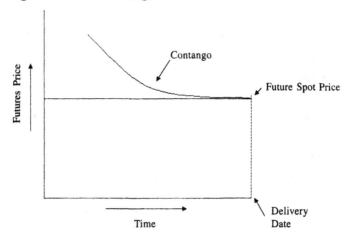

## Convergence

Convergence is the tendency of the futures price of a security to converge to the spot price at the maturity of the futures contract. If convergence did not occur, arbitrage opportunities would prevail, eventually causing the spot price and futures price to be equal at maturity.

## Converting Callable to Noncallable Bond

*See* Synthetic Noncallable Debt.

## Converting Noncallable to Callable Bond

*See* Synthetic Callable Debt.

## Covered Interest Rate Arbitrage

In a covered interest rate arbitrage (also known as *cash-and-carry arbitrage*) an investor borrows funds in domestic currency, buys foreign currency at the spot rate, and then invests these funds at the rate applicable for foreign funds for a fixed period. Simultaneously, the investor also enters into a forward or futures contract to sell the proceeds of the foreign funds on maturity of the investment and to buy domestic currency. An arbitrage profit is obtained because of the differential in the interest rate paid on the borrowed funds in domestic currency and the interest earned on the foreign funds investment.

## Cross Hedge

In a cross hedge, the requirements of the hedge and the hedge position do not exactly match. Thus the hedge and the underlying instrument are not perfectly correlated. A cross hedge may be the result of:

- Differences in timing of the requirement for the commodity and hedge contract period.
- Differences in the amount of commodity required and the size of the futures contracts available to hedge.
- Differences in the characteristics of the commodity being hedged and the characteristics of the commodity available through futures contract.

## Currency Swap

A currency swap is an over-the-counter contract in which two parties agree to exchange a series of payments denominated in two currencies. Principal payments are typically exchanged in two different currencies at the beginning and end of the contract.

For example, one party agrees to pay $1 million every year in exchange for the other party paying £1.5 million every year. In addition, each party may exchange the principal value of $10 million and £15 million respectively at the beginning of the contract and reverse the flows at maturity.

## Delta

The rate at which the price of an option changes relative to a change in the price of the underlying security is called delta.

Delta = Change in option price / Change in security price

The delta of a call option always lies between 0 and +1. The delta of a put option can be expressed as:

Delta of put = Delta of call − 1

It always lies between 0 and −1.

The delta goes down as the time to expiration increases. In the Black-Scholes formula delta is expressed as $N(d_1)$.

(*See also* Black-Scholes Option Pricing Model.)

## Delta-Neutral Portfolio

A delta-neutral portfolio is a risk-free combination of a long stock position and short calls. In a delta-neutral portfolio an infinitesimal change in the price of the stock has no effect on the portfolio.

The formula can be expressed as:

Portfolio = $-C + S$

where $C$ is the price of the call option on the stock and $S$ is the price of the stock.

The number of calls to sell on the stock position is determined by the following formula:

Number of calls to sell = $1/N(d_1)$

where $N(d_1)$ is the delta of the call.

A delta-neutral portfolio is important to risk management because it provides a baseline for option hedging strategies.

One of the weaknesses of the delta-neutral portfolio is that it needs constant rebalancing because, as the price of the underlying stock changes, the delta of the call option changes. As the delta changes, the number of calls to sell in order to maintain a risk-free position changes. This leads to high transaction costs.

## Derivatives

A derivative is a financial instrument whose value is derived from an underlying security. Derivatives serve many useful purposes in a financial market:

- They provide "market completeness," enabling investors to adjust their portfolio risks without trading the actual instruments.

- They provide a means of speculating on the market.

- They are a useful means of managing portfolio risk through hedging.

- They effectively control arbitrage by taking advantage of mispricing.

- They enhance trading efficiency by providing a means of taking or reducing exposure to the market without actually trading the instrument.

## European Option

*See* Options.

## Forward Contracts

Forward contracts are custom-made contracts to deliver or receive an asset at a future date at a predetermined price.

### ADVANTAGES

The main advantages of a forward contract are:

- It is flexible. The two parties entering into the contract can very much structure it to suit their needs.

- No up-front cash is required to enter into a forward contract;

- A forward contract need not be marked to market. Hence, price fluctuations do not affect the contract value, from a balance sheet point of view.

### DISADVANTAGES

The disadvantages of a forward contract are:

- It is illiquid.
- It exposes the parties to credit risk.
- It is not regulated.

(*See* Futures Contracts for the differences between forwards and futures.)

## Futures Contracts

A futures contract is a forward contract that is highly standardized and closely specified.

### ADVANTAGES

The advantages of a futures contract are:

- It is a standardized contract.
- It is traded on exchanges and therefore has a high level of availability and liquidity.
- Its performance is guaranteed by a clearinghouse.
- Futures markets are well regulated.

### DISADVANTAGES

The disadvantages of a futures contract are:

- There is little or no flexibility to customize the contract to meet the parties' needs.
- The contract has to be marked to market, thus affecting the books of accounts.

### *Differences with Forward Contracts*

Futures contracts differ from forward contracts in the following ways:

- Futures contracts are standardized, whereas forward contracts are customized.
- Futures contracts require daily marking to market; forward contracts do not require marking to market.
- Futures contracts require margin to be maintained; forward contracts do not require margin. (*See* Margins.)
- Futures contracts are traded on exchanges; forward contracts are negotiated over the counter and are custom made.
- A clearinghouse guarantees futures contract performance; forward contracts are not guaranteed.
- Futures contracts do not carry counterparty credit risk; forward contracts do expose the parties to counterparty risk.

### Differences with Options Contracts

Futures contracts differ from options contracts in the following ways:

- Options contracts require a premium to enter; futures contracts are practically "costless" to enter.

- Delivery or receipt of options contracts is at the option of the buyer; delivery or receipt of futures contract is not optional.

- Options contracts are not marked to market; futures contracts are marked to market and settled daily.

- In an options contract only the option writer (seller) is required to post margin, whereas in a futures contract both parties are required to post margin.

### Differences with Swaps

Futures contracts differ from swaps in the following ways:

- Swaps are negotiated in an over-the-counter market, whereas futures are traded on exchanges.

- Swaps are multiperiod contracts, whereas futures are single-period contracts.

- Swaps are not marked to market. Futures are marked to market daily.

- Swaps carry default risk; futures do not, since their performance is guaranteed by a clearinghouse.

(*See also* Forward Contracts; Options; Swaps.)

## Futures Contract Models

The six different models below help determine the appropriate level of hedging required for a bond portfolio.

### Basis Point Model

Under the basis point model, the number of contracts required for hedging is determined by using the relative price change in the futures for a basis point change in the spot.

### Conversion Factor Model

Futures contracts relating to T-bonds and T-notes require a conversion factor (CF) for computing the amount required to hedge a position. According to the CF model, each dollar of face value of cash instrument must be hedged with a dollar of face value of futures, factored by the CF for the instrument. Thus:

Hedge ratio = – (Face value of principal / Face value of futures) · (Conversion factor)

The negative sign indicates that the investor must sell futures when long on the cash instrument and buy futures when short on the cash instrument.

### Equal Dollar Method

*See* Face Value Naïve Model, below.

### Face Value Naïve Model

According to the face value naïve (FVN) model each dollar of face value of the instrument being hedged will be hedged with a dollar of face value of the futures contract. Under the FVN model the formula is:

Number of futures contracts = Number of bonds being hedged / Contract size

Note that the contract size for T-bond futures is usually 100 bonds or a face value of $100,000.

Although very simple, the FVN model ignores the differences in market value between the cash instrument being hedged and the futures positions used as hedge. This difference, in reality, could cause a poor hedge. The formula also neglects the impact of cash flow characteristics such as coupon and maturity that affect the duration of the cash and futures positions.

This model is also sometimes called the *equal dollar method.*

### Market Value Naïve Model

The market value naïve (MVN) model is similar to the face value naïve (FVN) model, except that it uses the market value of the cash instrument (instead of face value) and the futures contract to estimate the required number of contracts to hedge the position. Hence, for each dollar of market value of a cash instrument, a dollar of market value of futures contract is used to hedge.

The formula for computing the number of futures under this model is:

Number of futures contract = [(Price of bonds / Price of futures) · Number of bonds being hedged] / Contract size

Though this model considers the market value of the instrument and the futures contract, it still does not consider the price sensitivity of the two instruments.

### Minimum-Variance Model

*See* Regression Model, below.

### Price Sensitivity Model

The price sensitivity model takes into consideration the relative sensitivity of the bond being hedged and the sensitivity of the most deliverable bond used in the futures contract to changes in yields. The formula for determining the hedge ratio under this model is:

Hedge ratio = $(\text{PVBP}_B/\text{PVBP}_{MD}) \cdot (D_B/D_{MD}) \cdot CF_{MD}$

where

$\text{PVBP}_B$ = Price value basis point of the bond being hedged

$\text{PVBP}_{MD}$ = Price value basis point of the most deliverable bond underlying the futures contract

$D_B$ = Duration of the bond being hedged

$D_{MD}$ = Duration of the most deliverable bond

$CF_{MD}$ = Conversion factor of the most deliverable bond

### Regression Model

Under the regression model the relative number of futures contracts to sell is determined by regressing the percentage change in price of the security in the spot market against the percentage change in price of the security in the futures market. The slope coefficient of this regression gives the estimate for the hedge ratio.

This model is also called *minimum-variance model.*

## Gamma

Gamma is the rate at which the delta of an option changes as the price of the underlying security changes. It is expressed as:

Gamma = Change in delta / Change in price of underlying security

When an option is near the money, gamma tends to be a high value. A portfolio of derivatives with a high gamma will increase in value as the stock price increases.

(*See also* Moneyness.)

## Hedge Ratio

Hedge ratio helps determine the number of futures contracts required to hedge the long position of a certain number of units of a commodity or security being held.

(*See* Futures Contract Models for ways to compute the hedge ratio of a futures contract.)

## Hedging

The object of hedging is to reduce or eliminate a risky asset position by using derivatives such as futures, options, and swaps. (*See* Derivatives.)

A short hedge is used to cover the position of owning a commodity. It is used to eliminate uncertainty of the price for a commodity in the future when it is ready to be sold. A long hedge or an anticipatory hedge is used to eliminate price uncertainty for the commodity when it is needed at a future date.

Futures contracts are often used to hedge positions.

(*See* Futures Contract Models for ways to compute the hedge ratio of a futures contract.)

## Historical VAR

*See* Value at Risk (VAR).

## Implied Repo Rate

The implied repo rate is the interest rate that is implied in the price of a futures contract, when computed using a formula such as:

$$F = S [1 + (r_t/360)] - C_t$$

where

$F$ = Futures price

$S$ = Spot price

$r_t$ = Implied repo rate for the time period $t$

$C_t$ = Carrying cost for the time period $t$

$t$ = Time period

The implied repo rate itself can be expressed as:

$$r = \{[(F + C_t)/S] - 1\} (360/t)$$

## Interest Rate Cap and Floor

Interest rate caps and floors are financial instruments that help reduce the risk of exposure to excessive movements in interest rates.

Borrowers with a floating rate debt can buy an interest rate cap to protect themselves from a major rise in interest rates while retaining the full benefit of the downside movement of interest rates.

On the other hand, an interest rate floor protects the lender of a variable rate loan from a decline in interest rate below a limit.

## Interest Rate Collar

An interest rate collar places a maximum and a minimum value on the floating rate of interest. It is a combination of an interest rate cap and an interest rate floor.

Typically, an interest rate collar premium is less expensive than an interest rate cap premium (or interest rate floor premium), since the buyer gives up the benefit of any decline (or increase) in interest rate beyond the floor (or cap) limit.

## Interest Rate Futures Contracts

Interest rate futures contracts can be used to hedge against adverse movements in interest rates. Usually, Treasury bill futures or Eurobond futures are used to hedge against interest rate movements.

## Intrinsic Value

The intrinsic value of an option is the value that an investor can get if the option is exercised today.

For an *in-the-money* call option, the intrinsic value is the difference between the price of the underlying stock and the strike price of the option.

For an *in-the-money* put option, it is the difference between the strike price of the option and the price of the underlying stock.

For an *at-the-money* option and an *out-of-the-money* option, the intrinsic value is zero.

(*See also* Moneyness; Options.)

## Margins

Margins are funds that must be deposited with a clearinghouse before an investor or trader can trade on certain instruments (futures, covered options, etc.)

### Initial Margin

Initial margin is the first deposit required to be posted before an investor can trade on the instrument.

### Maintenance Margin

If the balance in the margin account falls below maintenance margin, the trader gets a margin call for additional funds.

### Variation Margin

Variation margin is the money required to be deposited into the account to bring it back up to the initial margin level.

## Moneyness

With options, moneyness is the state of being worthy of exercising in order to realize a profit. There are three states of moneyness: in the money, out of the money, and at the money. See Table 2-1.

### In the Money

An option that is in the money carries a positive return, and the exercise of the option at that time will give the holder of the option a profit.

### Out of the Money

An option that is out of the money carries a negative return, and the exercise of the option at that time will give the holder of the option a loss.

### At the Money

An option that is at the money carries neither a positive nor a negative return.

For an option, different states of moneyness prevail at different levels of delta, vega, and theta. Table 2-2 provides a summary of the values of these factors and their respective moneyness. (*See also* Delta; Theta; and Vega.)

## Most Deliverable Bond

In a Treasury bond futures contract, when the contract expires, the party that is to deliver the bond will deliver the

### Table 2-1 States of Moneyness

|  | Out of the money | At the money | In the money |
|---|---|---|---|
| Calls | $S_t < X$ | $S_t = X$ | $S_t > X$ |
| Puts | $S_t > X$ | $S_t = X$ | $S_t < X$ |

$S_t$ is the price of the stock at time $t$ and $X$ is the exercise price of the option.

## Table 2-2 Moneyness of Delta, Vega, and Theta

|  | Out of the money | At the money | In the money |
|---|---|---|---|
| Delta of a call | 0 |  | +1 |
| Delta of a put | 0 |  | −1 |
| Vega | 0 | Max | 0 |
| Theta | 0 | Max (negative) | 0 |

When the delta of a call is 0 or close to 0, the option is out of the money. When the delta of a call is +1 or close to +1, the option is in-the-money.

cheapest bond available in the market that meets the requirements of the contract. This bond is known as the most deliverable bond.

Bond managers use the implied repo rate (lowest price) to identify the most deliverable bond. The bond that has the highest implied repo rate and that meets the requirements of the contract is then selected.

### Options

An options contract gives the buyer the right, but not the obligation, to buy or sell a specific security at a specific price on or before a specific date.

An American option can be exercised any time from the date of purchase until the time of expiration. A European option can be exercised only on the date of expiration.

A bermuda option is a combination of both the American and European options. It can be exercised on any one of a number of prespecified dates.

(*See also* Intrinsic Value; Time Value.)

The price of an option is influenced by the following factors:

- Strike price (or exercise price) of the option relative to the stock price ($X$)
- Price of the underlying security (delta)
- Volatility of the price of the underlying security (vega)

- Time to expiration of the option (theta)
- Level of prevailing interest rates (rho)
- Dividends on the underlying stock ($D$)
- Type of option (American / European)

(*See* Futures Contracts for the differences between options and futures.)

## Options Strategies

Some of the options strategies commonly deployed are described below.

### Bear Spread

A bear spread can be created by using call options as follows:

- Buy a call with a high strike price.
- Sell a call with a low strike price.

All other parameters of the calls remain the same.

Such a strategy is deployed when the price of the stock is expected to fall. This strategy can be executed using put options instead of calls.

See Figure 2-3.

## Figure 2–3   Bear Spread (Using Call Options)

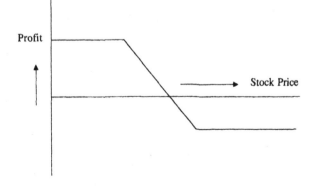

### Bull Spread

A bull spread strategy can be created using call options as follows:

- Buy a call with a low strike price;
- Sell a call with a higher strike price.

All other parameters of the call remain the same.

This is a useful strategy to adopt if the price of the underlying stock is expected to rise. The strategy can be executed using put options instead of calls.

See Figure 2-4.

### Butterfly Spread

A butterfly spread strategy requires four calls or four puts.

A long butterfly position on a particular stock can be created by taking the following positions with the same exercise date:

- Buy one call with a high strike price.
- Sell two calls with a medium strike price.
- Buy one call with a low strike price.

A short butterfly strategy can be created as follows:

- Sell one call with a high strike price.
- Buy two calls with a medium strike price.
- Sell one call with a low strike price.

## Figure 2–4   Bull Spread (Using Call Options)

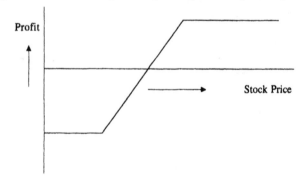

Put options can be used to create similar positions that give rise to the same effect. A butterfly spread is useful when the stock trades within a narrow range.

See Figure 2-5.

### Condor Spread

A condor spread can be constructed by using either four call or four puts in the following way:

- Buy one call with a low strike price.
- Sell one call with a higher strike price.
- Sell one call with a further higher strike price.
- Buy one call with an even higher strike price.

The above describes a long condor spread. Replacing the "buy" with "sell" and "sell" with "buy" creates a short condor spread.

The condor spread is useful when the stock price remains within a defined range, leaving the portfolio exposed to only a small risk if the stock becomes more volatile.

See Figure 2-6.

## Figure 2-5   Butterfly Spread (Using Calls)

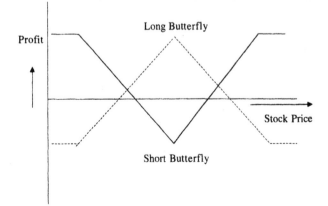

## Figure 2–6   Condor Spread (Using Calls)

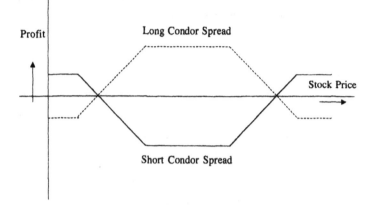

## Covered Call

A covered call is a call option that is sold (written) by the owner of the stock. Covered calls are written by the owner to earn a premium and enhance the return on the stock.

The advantage of a covered call is the premium earned on the call, but the downside is that the upside potential is limited if the stock price were to indeed rise beyond expectations.

Covered calls are useful when the stock price is stable.

See Figure 2-7.

## Figure 2–7   Covered Call

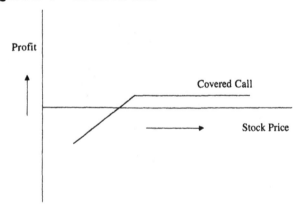

### Naked Call

A naked call strategy involves buying or selling a call option without owning the underlying stock.

Owning (buying) a naked call can be profitable if you expect the stock price to increase. Selling a naked call is useful when you expect the stock price to decline.

See Figure 2-8.

### Naked Put

A naked put strategy involves buying or selling a put option without owning the underlying stock.

Buying a naked put will pay off when the stock price declines, and selling a naked put will pay off when stock price increases.

See Figure 2-9.

### Protective Put

Buying a put option on a stock you own is a protective put. It is a defensive strategy aimed at insuring the value of the portfolio. It helps protect against the downside, while retaining the upside.

Buying calls on an index and investing the balance in T-bills can create a synthetic protective put.

See Figure 2-10.

## Figure 2–8   Naked Call

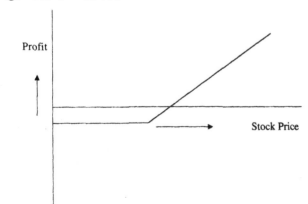

## Figure 2–9  Naked Put

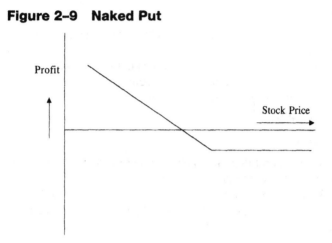

(*See* Put-Call Parity Theorem to derive an equation for a synthetic protective put.)

### *Straddle*

Buying both a call and a put option on the same stock with the same exercise price and the same expiration date is known as a straddle.

## Figure 2–10  Protective Put

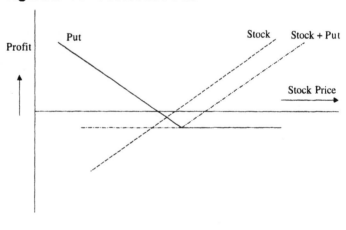

This is a good strategy to employ when you are uncertain about the direction of movement of the stock price, but you are confident that there will be a price movement in the near future. The strategy will not perform well if the stock price remains stable.

See Figure 2-11.

### Strangle

A strangle strategy consists of a put and a call as follows:

- Buy a put with a strike price below the price of the underlying asset.

- Buy a call with a strike price above the price of the underlying asset.

This is a good strategy to adopt if you are uncertain about the direction of movement of the stock price, but you are confident that there will be a large price movement in the near future. This strategy will not perform well if the stock price remains stable or trades within a narrow range.

See Figure 2-12.

Table 2-3 provides a summary of the various options strategies and when to use them.

## Figure 2-11 Straddle

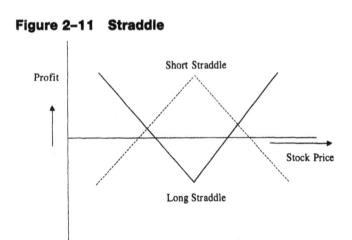

## Figure 2–12   Strangle

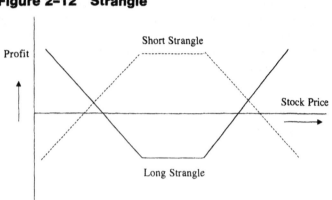

## Table 2-3   When to Use What Options Strategy

| Security Performance Expectation | Preferred Option Strategy |
| --- | --- |
| Falling prices | Buy naked put |
| Falling prices | Adopt bear spread strategy |
| Rising prices | Buy naked call |
| Rising prices | Adopt bull spread strategy |
| Stable or falling prices | Sell naked call |
| Stable or falling prices | Sell covered call |
| Stable or rising prices | Sell naked put |
| Stable prices | Sell straddle |
| Stable prices | Sell strangle |
| Stable prices | Adopt long butterfly spread |
| Stable prices | Adopt condor spread |
| Very volatile prices | Buy strangle |
| Volatile prices | Buy straddle |
| Volatile prices | Adopt short butterfly spread |
| Volatile prices | Sell condor spread |

## Parametric VAR

*See* Value at Risk (VAR).

## Portfolio Insurance

A portfolio can be insured against losses by using derivatives. Two popular portfolio insurance strategies involve futures and puts.

- Selling futures on a stock reduces exposure to that stock and helps avoid negative returns.

- Buying protective puts provides insurance against losses in a portfolio.

Some of the differences between these two approaches to portfolio insurance are:

- Futures provide a symmetrical payoff, whereas puts have asymmetrical payoffs. See Figure 2-13 (a) and (b).

- Futures require constant rebalancing and hence call for a dynamic hedging strategy. Puts need only be held after purchase, with little rebalancing and monitoring.

- Futures are marked to market daily, producing cash flow differences over time. Puts are not marked to market.

- Futures are costless to enter. Puts require a premium.

## Figure 2–13(a)   Symmetrical Payoff of Futures

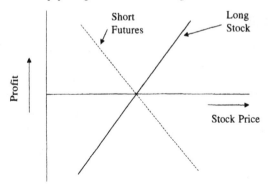

## Figure 2–13(b)  Asymmetrical Payoff of Puts

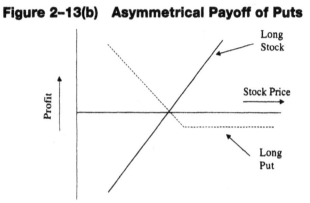

### Price Discovery

The price of a futures contract for a commodity provides valuable information regarding the expected price of the commodity in the future. Thus the futures market aids in "price discovery" of securities—the gleaning of information about future cash market prices through the futures market.

### Put Swaption (or Payer Swaption)

*See* Swaptions.

### Put-Call Parity Theorem

The put-call parity theorem establishes a relationship between put and call options. It is based on the fact that a call option can be synthetically created by owning a put option and the underlying asset.

The put-call parity theorem can be expressed as:

$$P = C + X/(1 + i)^n - S$$

where

    $P$ = Price of a put on a particular stock

    $C$ = price of a call on that stock

$X$ = Exercise price

$i$ = Prevailing interest rate

$n$ = Period of the option

$S$ = Current stock price

## Reverse Cash-and-Carry Arbitrage

In a reverse cash-and-carry arbitrage a trader takes advantage of the differential between the prevailing interest rates and the implied repo rate in a futures contract. In other words, a reverse cash-and-carry arbitrage opportunity exists when the futures contract is underpriced and/or market interest rates are higher than that implied by the futures price.

The steps of a reverse cash-and-carry arbitrage are as follows.

At time 0:

- Sell goods short.
- Lend proceeds of short sales for time $t$.
- Buy futures contract to take delivery of goods at time $t$.

At time $t$:

- Collect proceeds from the loan.
- Pay for goods and accept delivery against the futures contract.
- Deliver goods against short sale.
- Pocket the difference.

(*See also* Cash-and-Carry Arbitrage; Covered Interest Rate Arbitrage; Implied Repo Rate.)

## Rho

The rate at which the price of an option changes relative to a change in the level of interest rates is known as rho. The formula is as follows:

Rho = Change in option price/Change in risk-free interest rate

## Shortening or Lengthening T-Bill Maturity Using Futures

Selling T-bill futures can synthetically shorten the maturity of a security, since the security is delivered on maturity of the futures. Similarly, buying T-bill futures can artificially lengthen the maturity of a security.

## Stock Index Futures

Stock index futures are futures contracts based on a stock index such as the S&P 500. Index futures can be used to alter an equity portfolio in the following ways:

- Creating a synthetic T-bill from an equity portfolio.
- Creating a synthetic equity portfolio.
- Adjusting the risk level (beta) of an equity portfolio.
- Altering the weighting of an equity portfolio to different types of stocks.

The value of stock index futures can be computed by using the formula:

$$F = S(1 + r_{fp}) + C_p - D_p$$

where

$F$ = Futures price of the stock index

$S$ = Spot price of the stock index

$r_{fp}$ = Risk-free interest rate

$C_p$ = Carrying cost (usually zero for stocks)

$D_p$ = Dividend received during the period

## Swaps

A swap is an agreement between two or more parties to exchange a set of cash flows over a period in the future. It is a customized risk management vehicle.

The pricing of swaps can be constructed using forward rates. Swaps can be seen as a series of forward rate agreements. Hence, a swap's fixed rate is theoretically equal to the average of the prevailing forward rates over the period of the swap. It is necessary for this theorem to hold in order to prevent arbitrage.

Swaps carry the following risks:

- Measurement risk—the risk of hedging too much or too little.

- Basis risk—the risk caused by a mismatch between the timing of inflows and outflows (receipts and payments).

- Credit risk—the risk of default by the counterparty.

- Mismatch risk—especially from a dealer's perspective, if the dealer is unable to find a counterparty willing to take the opposite position on a swap.

(*See also* Forward Contracts; Hedging.)

### Interest Rate Swap

An interest rate swap is an agreement between two parties to exchange a series of interest payment cash flows, for a certain period of time, based on a certain notional principal amount.

Typically, in an interest rate swap, the principal amount is not exchanged. Only the net interest payments are exchanged. Interest rate swaps can be used to convert a fixed interest payment obligation into a variable interest payment obligation and vice versa.

An interest rate swap has the following characteristics:

- Periodic exchange of interest payments takes place between the contracting parties.

- The proceeds of the swap are settled on a "net basis"; that is, the party that owes the greater of the two interest amounts due on the settlement date pays the difference in the amounts due.

- Interest rate swaps are entered into for the same currency.

- Principal amounts of the swap contract are not exchanged.

See Figure 2-14.

## Figure 2–14   Interest Rate Swap

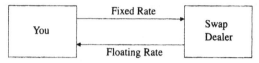

### Currency Swap

A currency swap has the following characteristics:

- Periodic exchange of interest payments takes place between the counterparties.

- At each settlement date both parties pay their due amounts in full; the settlement is not "netted off."

- Each party pays in a different currency.

- Principal amounts are exchanged at the commencement and maturity of the contract.

See Figure 2-15.

### Equity Swap

An equity swap helps create synthetic equity exposures. The net exposure to an equity swap position is the total return on the equity index.

See Figure 2-16.

(*See* Futures Contracts for the differences between swaps and futures.)

## Figure 2–15   Currency Swap

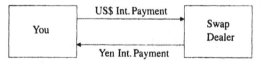

Only interest payments are shown.

## Figure 2-16   Equity Swap

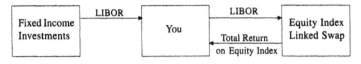

LIBOR = London Interbank Offered Rate.

## Swaptions

A swaption is an option to enter into a swap at preset terms on or before a certain date.

A put swaption (also called a *payer's swaption*) gives the owner the right to pay a fixed rate and receive a floating rate. It is useful when interest rates are expected to rise.

A call swaption gives the owner the right to receive a fixed rate and pay a floating rate. It is useful when interest rates are expected to decline.

Although swaptions give the owner the benefit of having the option to enter into a swap, they also carry some disadvantages:

- Swaptions are typically illiquid. Hence, availability and liquidity could be an issue.

- They carry a high transaction cost because of their limited availability.

- They carry counterparty credit risk.

- The premium of the option on the swap reduces the total return.

- Swaptions complicate performance measurement of the investments.

## Synthetic Callable Debt (Using Swaps)

Say you have issued a fixed rate, noncallable debt. You suspect that interest rates are likely to fall. So you want to have the option to call the debt and convert it into a floating rate debt.

## Figure 2–17  Synthetic Callable Debt (Using Swaps)

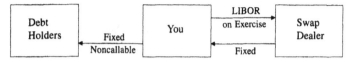

LIBOR = London Interbank Offered Rate.

You can achieve this using a call swaption as described in Figure 2-17.

The advantage of the call swaption in creating synthetic callable debt is that, if you had issued callable debt, you would call the bonds and reissue them at a lower rate when interest rates fell. In so doing, you would incur the cost of liquidating the bonds as well as reissuing them.

The call swaption gives you the right to refinance the debt at a lower floating rate without actually liquidating the bonds and reissuing them.

### Synthetic Equity Portfolio (Using Stock Index Futures)

A synthetic equity portfolio gives the investor exposure to the stock market without actually buying stocks.

After determining the desired level of exposure to the stock market the investor can purchase an adequate number of S&P 500 futures contracts. This will, in effect, create a synthetic portfolio that replicates the performance of the S&P 500.

### Synthetic Fixed Rate Debt (Using Futures)

If a firm desires to convert its floating rate loan to a fixed rate loan in the fear of rising interest rates, it can create a synthetic fixed rate loan using futures contracts.

By selling Eurodollar futures, the firm can hedge against rising interest rates, since when rates rise, the futures contracts price will fall and the party that has sold the contracts short will benefit. This gain will be offset by the losses on the floating rate debt.

## Synthetic Fixed Rate Debt (Using Swaps)

If you are currently paying floating rate interest and you fear that interest rates are likely to rise, you will want to switch to a fixed rate debt. You can easily do so by entering into a swap, exchanging your floating rate debt for a fixed rate debt.

See Figure 2-18.

## Synthetic Floating Rate Debt (Using Futures)

When a firm is exposed to interest rate risk from a fixed rate loan, it may desire to convert the loan into a floating rate debt when interest rates are falling. This can be achieved by buying Eurodollar futures contracts. The firm will lose from a decline in interest rate (since the fixed rate debt is relatively expensive) even while it gains from the futures contracts as its prices increase. These two (loss on the fixed rate debt and gain from the futures contract) offset each other, thus giving the firm the effect of a synthetic floating rate debt.

## Synthetic Floating Rate Debt (Using Swaps)

Suppose you are paying a fixed rate on a debt and you fear that interest rates are likely to drop. Therefore, you want to switch your fixed rate debt for floating rate debt. You can achieve this by entering into a swap to create a synthetic floating rate debt.

See Figure 2-19.

## Figure 2–18   Synthetic Fixed Rate Debt (Using Swaps)

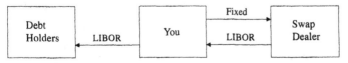

LIBOR = London Interbank Offered Rate.

## Figure 2–19   Synthetic Floating Rate Debt (Using Swaps)

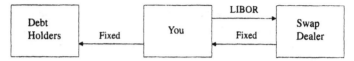

LIBOR = London Interbank Offered Rate.

## Synthetic Noncallable Debt (Using Swaps)

Say you have issued a callable bond and paid a premium for the call option embedded in the bond. Interest rates are stable and you fear that the option embedded in the bond will expire worthless.

You can convert this callable bond into a noncallable bond by selling a call option and collecting a premium on the swaption. If the swaption is exercised, you can call the existing bond, issue floating rate notes (FRNs), receive a floating rate on the FRNs, and pay a fixed rate on the swap (entered through the swaption).

See Figure 2-20.

(*See also* Swaptions; Synthetic Floating Rate Debt.)

## Synthetic T-Bill from an Equity Portfolio (Using Stock Index Futures)

If a portfolio manager expects the stock market to perform poorly and therefore have a negative impact on an equity

## Figure 2–20   Synthetic Noncallable Debt (Using Swaps)

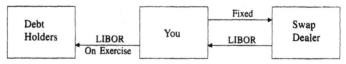

LIBOR = London Interbank Offered Rate.

portfolio, the manager can enter into a stock index futures contract such that the combined return on the portfolio and the futures contract mimic the return on a T-bill.

The manager can do this by selling an adequate number of S&P 500 futures contracts such that the gains on the futures contracts (due to decline in the stock market) will be offset by the losses in the portfolio, thus providing a virtual risk-free return, as with a T-bill.

Using this strategy, a manager can quickly convert the equity portfolio into a synthetic T-bill without actually incurring the cost of selling the portfolio and buying T-bills.

## Tailing the Hedge

Tailing the hedge is the process by which a trader adjusts the hedge, almost daily, to compensate for the interest that can be earned (or paid) on daily settlement of profits (or losses) on the futures contracts.

This process is especially important in interest rate futures hedging, since a possible positive correlation between interest rates and futures price can cause significant variation in the size of the hedge.

(*See also* Hedging.)

## Theta

The rate at which the price of an option changes relative to a change in the time to expiration of the option is called theta. The formula is as follows:

Theta = Change in option price / Change in time to expiration of the option

For example, a theta of 0.04 means that each day the option value decreases by $0.04. Theta increases when an option is at the money and as the time to maturity of an option comes closer.

## Time Value

The value inherent in an option because its intrinsic value may change in the future is known as time value. It is the value in excess of the intrinsic value and hence it is also called the *premium* on the option.

This time value is dependent upon:

- Volatility of the underlying security
- Level of interest rates
- Time until expiration
- Dividend paid on the underlying stock

## Value at Risk (VAR)

Value at risk (VAR) is a risk measure of how much the value of a portfolio could decline, in a given period of time, with a given probability. The calculation of VAR requires a common measurement unit, a time horizon, and a probability level.

VAR is useful in measuring risks that are quantifiable, such as interest rate risk, currency risk, and credit risk. It is also useful in measuring the risk of frequently traded securities for which market data are available, such as bonds, stocks, and options.

VAR is not useful in measuring nonquantifiable risks such as operational and legal risks.

The formula is as follows:

VAR = Mean return – (Standard deviation) · (Z score)

where the Z score is given by the following data:

| Confidence Interval | Z Score |
|---|---|
| 90% | 1.28 |
| 95% | 1.65 |
| 97.5% | 1.96 |
| 99% | 2.33 |

There are three different approaches to computing VAR: parametric VAR, historical VAR, and simulated VAR.

### Parametric VAR

Parametric VAR is based on the parameters of distribution—that is, the estimate of variance-covariance matrix of asset returns.

Parametric VAR assumes the following:

- The distribution of asset returns are normal.
- Returns are serially independent (i.e., today's return is not dependent upon yesterday's return).
- Volatility change is estimated by exponential weighting of observations.
- In order to estimate VAR only the parameters of distribution are required.

The advantage of parametric VAR is that it is simple to use—all you need to compute VAR is the mean and standard deviation of returns.

The disadvantages are that it assumes that returns follow a normal distribution pattern and that they are serially independent. Both assumptions do not hold in the real world.

### Historical VAR

Historical VAR is calculated by plotting the historical returns and taking the lowest returns in the historical data.

Historical VAR does not make any assumptions on volatility of returns, covariances, or the shape of the returns distribution. However, it lacks flexibility and cannot be used to test sensitivity of variance by using different values for volatility and covariances. Also, probability distributions of returns are not stable over time. Hence, the use of historical returns to predict future returns is not entirely reliable.

### Simulated VAR

Simulated VAR can be computed by simulating returns on the current portfolio, using actual past values.

Simulation is useful for large or complex portfolios and provides the ability to view the portfolio returns under different probability scenarios. Simulation, of course, carries "model risk"—that is, risk of misspecification of model parameters.

### Limitations of VAR

VAR is popular as a risk measure because it is easy to understand, since it presents risk as one aggregate estimate in dollar terms. However, it carries a number of limitations:

- VAR is only an approximation and not an accurate value of loss predicted.

- VAR is useful to estimate losses for short periods, such as a day, a week, or at most a month; it is not recommended for longer periods.

- VAR is dependent on the model and the data used.

- In the case of historical VAR, historical data may not hold in the future.

- VAR is heavily dependent on the assumptions.

- VAR computations need constant updating to reflect current distribution patterns.

- VAR is not recommended in isolation. It should be used along with other risk measures.

## Variation Margin

*See* Margins.

## Vega

The rate at which the price of an option changes relative to a change in the volatility of the underlying security is known as Vega.

The formula is as follows:

Vega = Change in option price/Change in volatility of underlying security

For example, a Vega of 0.08 means that for every 1 percent increase in volatility in the underlying instrument, the option price increases by $0.08.

Options are most sensitive to changes in volatility (i.e., have high vegas) when they are at the money. As time to maturity increases, vega increases. Deep out-of-the-money or in-the-money options have low sensitivity to changes in volatility (low vega).

# SECTION 3

# Economics

## Absolute Advantage

Economically a country is said to have an absolute advantage if that country can produce more of a good than another country with the same amount of resources. The advantage is derived from its inherent natural resources and/or previous experience.

(*See also* Comparative Advantage.)

## Accounting Profit

*See* Economic Profit.

## Adaptive-Expectations Theory

According to adaptive-expectations theory, analysts base their future expectations on the actual outcomes experienced in the immediate past. That is, the immediate past has a significant bearing on the immediate future.

For example, inflation projections for next year will tend to be largely based on actual inflation experienced in the past few years, rather than on the long-run inflation rate.

(*See also* Rational Expectations Hypothesis.)

## Automatic Stabilizers

Fiscal policies that tend to automatically produce a budget deficit during a recession and a budget surplus during an inflationary boom are called automatic stabilizers. Three of the most popular automatic stabilizers are unemployment compensation, corporate profit tax, and progressive income tax.

Here is how stabilizers work:

- During recessionary periods unemployment tends to rise. The government increases its unemployment compensation, thus widening the budget deficit.

- During boom periods, unemployment tends to decrease and the expenditure to the government under this policy declines, thus generating a balanced budget or surplus. Similarly, a corporate profit tax brings in additional revenues during periods of boom, leading to a budget surplus.

## Balance of Payments

A country's balance of payments (BOP) provides a summary of all economic transactions of that country with all other countries with which it has a trading relationship, for a specific period of time, usually a year.

It reflects all payments and liabilities to foreigners and all payments and obligations due from foreigners. Thus, BOP provides a snapshot of the financial health of a country with respect to its foreign trading and currency positions.

## Business Cycle

The business cycle maps the characteristic fluctuation in the general level of economic activity of a country over a period of time. It is usually measured by economic variables such as rate of unemployment and changes in real gross domestic product.

A typical business cycle follows the pattern of business peak (or boom), contraction, recession, and expansion.

See Figure 3-1.

---

### Factoid on the Business Cycle

Peaks and troughs in stock prices have typically preceded turning points in the business cycle. The pattern indicates that the stock market is a leading indicator of business cycle changes.

---

## Classical Economists

Economists such as Adam Smith and John Maynard Keynes, who focused on economic efficiency and production as the key to stability and growth, are known as classical economists. They believed that prices and wages would decline quickly enough during a recession to bring back full employment in a short period of time.

## Comparative Advantage

A nation is said to have a comparative advantage if it can gain by producing a good more cheaply than another country (i.e., at a lower opportunity cost), and then exchanging that product for goods for which the nation has a higher opportunity cost.

(*See also* Absolute Advantage.)

## Figure 3-1   Business Cycle

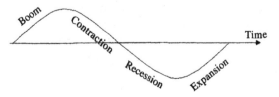

## Consensus Forecasting

*See* Forecasting Methods.

## Consumer Price Index

The Consumer Price Index (CPI) is an index based on the comparison of the prices of a typical basket of goods measured during one period against the prices of the same set of goods in another period.

## Crowding-out Effect

Large fiscal deficits compel a government to finance the debt by borrowing from the market. When a government comes to borrow from its market, investors tend to prefer the risk-free investment of the government's securities to private borrowings. This tends to crowd out the private borrowers, who have to offer a higher premium over the government issues in order to attract investors.

## Deadweight Loss

Deadweight loss is the net loss to an economic system resulting from a specific economic decision. It reflects an economic inefficiency.

See Figure 3-2.

## Economic Profit

Economic profit is the difference between total revenues and total costs, including both the implicit and explicit costs.

### Differences with Accounting Profit

Accounting profit does not consider the opportunity cost of the firm's equity capital and, therefore, generally overstates economic profit. Economic profit, on the other hand, takes into consideration opportunity costs resulting from production of a good or service.

Accounting profit is based on market transactions, while

## Figure 3–2   Deadweight Loss

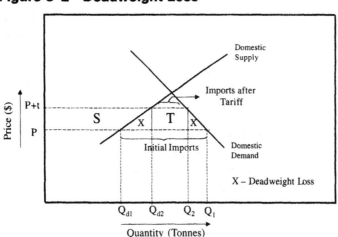

economic profit is based on opportunity costs. Finally, only explicit costs are considered in calculating accounting profit, whereas both explicit and implicit costs are included in computing economic profit.

## Forecasting Methods

There are three types of forecasting methods: consensus, multiple-scenario, and historical.

All three forecasting methods have value, but they seldom provide actionable conclusions. Hence, for an analyst, judgment is still the key.

### Consensus Forecasting

Consensus forecasting attempts to determine the "mind of the market" by collecting, averaging, and studying judgments of many analysts, economists, and other market players.

#### ADVANTAGE

- Consensus forecasting provides the collective wisdom of many experts from different perspectives.

**DISADVANTAGES**

- Consensus forecasting is subject to the possibility of either accepting an incorrect market judgment or rejecting a correct market judgment.

- It has missed critical turning points in economic trends or indicators (such as the 1982 market downturn and the 1990–91 recession).

### Multiple-Scenario Forecasting

Multiple-scenario forecasting (MSF) attempts to identify different possible economic "states" and develops alternate scenarios for various key economic variables. A probability of occurrence of each state is also estimated and a most likely scenario outcome is determined.

**ADVANTAGES**

- MSF forces the analyst to focus on key variables and assumptions.

- It can be subjected to sensitivity testing that can help examine the outcomes during extreme conditions.

- It can pick up turning points missed in consensus forecasting.

- It can prevent "groupthink."

**DISADVANTAGE**

- MSF can result in "analysis paralysis" with the analyst attempting to estimate endless possible scenarios.

### Historical Forecasting

Historical forecasting uses past data to predict the future.

**ADVANTAGE**

- Historical forecasting provides a norm or a basis for the future.

**DISADVANTAGE**

- The past is not always a prologue to the future.

## Forecasts

There are two types of forecasts: cyclical forecasts and secular forecasts.

### Cyclical Forecasts

Cyclical forecasts are near-term forecasts that extend into the next four to eight quarters. These are demand forecasts that are influenced by factors such as change in income (profits) and expenditure patterns and levels, as well as monetary and fiscal policies.

### Secular Forecasts

Secular forecasts are longer-term projections well into the next five to ten years. These are supply-based projections and are extensively based on demographic patterns, capital formation, technological innovations, increased productivity levels, expected inflation levels, and the international political and economic environment. Such forecasts are conditional and subject to realization of many assumptions.

## Fractional Reserve Banking

The fractional reserve system of banking allows banks to hold reserves that are less than their total deposits. This system facilitates credit creation through the multiplier effect.

## Full Employment

An economy is said to have full employment when almost the entire labor force is employed, and the remaining unemployment is due solely to structural conditions of the economy, information nonavailability, and dynamic changes in the economy.

The United States is said to have full employment when 94 to 95 percent of the labor force is employed.

## Gross Domestic Product (GDP)

GDP is the total value of all end products and services produced domestically by a country during a specific period, usually a year.

Nominal GDP is expressed at current prices, while real GDP takes into consideration changes in prices of the items included in computing GDP. The formula is as follows:

Real GDP = Nominal GDP / GDP deflator

## Herfindahl Index

The Herfindahl Index is used to measure the concentration of an industry in order to identify monopoly or oligopoly industries.

It is calculated by squaring the percentage of market share of each company in the industry and then summing the squares. The index can range from zero to 10,000. The higher the index, the more the industry is considered a monopoly. It is used by the U.S. Justice Department in adjudicating antitrust cases.

If there are $n$ firms in the market, then the Herfindahl Index ($H$) can be computed as:

$$H = S_1^2 + S_2^2 + S_3^2 + \ldots + S_n^2$$

where $S_1, S_2 \ldots S_n$ are the market shares of firms 1 to $n$.

## Historical Forecasting

*See* Forecasting Methods.

## Index of Leading Indicators

The index of leading indicators is based on economic indicators that tend to precede a turning point in the business cycle, such as a recession or an economic expansion.

Table 3-1 lists some select leading, coincident, and lagging indicators, according to the National Bureau of Economic Research (NBER).

## Interest Rate Parity

Interest Rate Parity theorem states that the currency values of different countries will change relative to each other in order to keep the real rates of interest across the countries equal. This is represented by the formula:

## Table 3-1   Economic Indicators

**Leading Indicators**

| |
|---|
| Index of stock prices, 500 common stocks |
| M2 money supply (in 1982 dollars) |
| Index of raw private housing units authorized by local building permits |
| Contracts and orders for plant and equipment (in 1982 dollars) |

**Coincident Indicators**

| |
|---|
| Employees on nonagricultural payrolls |
| Index of industrial production |
| Manufacturing and trade sales (in 1982 dollars) |

**Lagging Indicators**

| |
|---|
| Commercial and industrial loans outstanding (in 1982 dollars) |
| Ratio of manufacturing and trade inventories to sales (in 1982 dollars) |
| Average prime rate charged by banks |

$$S_2 = S_1 \cdot [(1 + r_d)/(1 + r_f)]$$

where

$S_1$ = Current value of the domestic currency (expressed as the amount required for one unit of foreign currency)

$S_2$ = Expected future value of the domestic currency

$r_d$ = Rate of interest in the domestic country

$r_f$ = Rate of interest in the foreign country

## J-Curve Effect

When a country's currency depreciates, theoretically, its current account deficit should shrink as imports fall and exports rise. However, in reality the current account deficit tends to widen initially before it shrinks, creating the J-curve effect. This is due to the short-run inelasticity of demand of both imports and exports. In the long run, both tend to be elastic and the currency depreciation will tend to bridge the current account deficit.

See Figure 3-3.

## Figure 3-3    J-Curve Effect

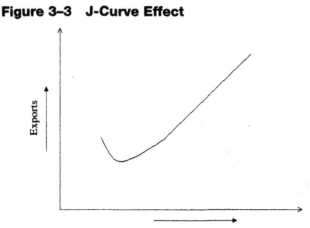

Currency Value (per unit of foreign currency)

### Law of Comparative Advantage

*See* Comparative Advantage.

### Law of Diminishing Marginal Utility

Marginal utility is the additional utility received by a person from the consumption of an additional unit of a good within a given time period.

The law of diminishing marginal utility states that, as the consumption of a commodity increases, the marginal utility derived from consuming more of that commodity will eventually decline.

### Money Supply

Money supply in a financial system is measured by three indicators: M1, M2, and M3.

#### M1 Money Supply

M1 is the sum of:

- Currency in circulation (including coins)
- Demand deposits

- Checking accounts
- Traveler's checks

### M2 Money Supply

M2 is M1 plus:

- Savings and time deposits (accounts of less than $100,000)
- Money market mutual fund shares
- Money market deposit accounts
- Overnight loans from customers to commercial banks
- Overnight Eurodollar deposits held by U.S. residents

### M3 Money Supply

M3 is M2 plus:

- Time deposits (accounts of over $100,000)
- Longer-term loans of customers to commercial banks and other institutions

## Monopolistic Competition

Characteristics of a market with monopolistic competition are:

- Large number of independent sellers
- Each producing a differentiated product
- A market with low barriers to entry
- Competitors exhibiting "price searcher" behavior

The construction industry and retail sales industry are good examples of monopolistic competition. Unlike a pure monopoly, in which barriers to entry are high, monopolistic competitors have low barriers to entry.

## Multiple-Scenario Forecasting

*See* Forecasting Methods.

## Neoclassical Economists

Neoclassical economists believe that market forces will push the economy to full-employment equilibrium and that macroeconomic policy is an ineffective tool to control economic instability.

According to these economists, when the government finances its budget with debt, consumers will automatically reduce their consumption in order to increase their savings, since higher taxes might be required to cover the debt financing.

## Oligopoly

In an oligopoly a small number of sellers make up the entire industry. Since there are only a few participants in an oligopolistic market, decisions of one seller often affect the other sellers. Hence, sellers watch each other's moves closely.

Because economies of scale are important in order to operate profitably in an oligopolistic market, they serve as a barrier to new entrants into the market.

## Phillips Curve

The Phillips curve illustrates the relationship between the rate of change of inflation and the rate of unemployment.

See Figure 3-4.

## Price Elasticity of Demand

Price elasticity of demand (PED) shows the effect of change in price on the demand for that product. It is given by the formula:

PED = % Change in the quantity of a product demanded /
% Change in the price causing the change in quantity

A product tends to be price inelastic if it has only a limited number of good substitutes.

## Figure 3–4    Phillips Curve

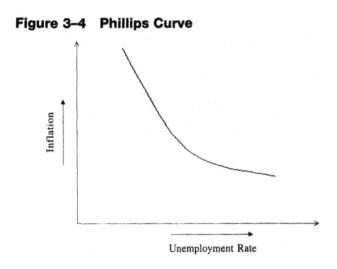

Unemployment Rate

## Purchasing Power Parity (PPP)

### Law of One Price

The law of one price states that, assuming competitive markets and no transportation costs or tariffs, the real price of a good, measured in a common currency, will be the same across all countries.

Of course, the law does not hold in practice because of unrealistic assumptions such as no transportation costs and no tariffs.

### Absolute PPP

Assuming there are no transportation costs or barriers to trade, according to absolute purchasing power parity, the same basket of goods, when measured in a common currency, should have the same price in all countries.

Under absolute PPP, the equilibrium exchange rate between two currencies is the rate that equalizes the prices of a basket of goods between two countries.

Absolute PPP does not hold in the real world because there *are* impediments to trade, and the basket of goods used to measure prices in different countries could be different.

### Relative PPP

According to relative PPP, the exchange rate movements between two currencies reflect differences in price changes of a basket of goods (inflation rates) between the two countries.

Hence, a country experiencing a high inflation rate will find its currency depreciating in value relative to a country with a low inflation rate. The formula is as follows:

$$S_1 = S_0 \left[(1 + I_f)/(1 + I_d)\right] - 1$$

where

$S_1$ = Value of foreign currency per unit of domestic currency

$S_0$ = Value of currency of the domestic country

$I_f$ = Inflation in the foreign country

$I_d$ = Inflation in the domestic country

## Pure Competition

A pure competition market is characterized by a large number of small firms producing a homogenous product in an industry that has no barriers to entry or exit.

Purely competitive firms are "price takers," since they have very little control over the price they can charge.

## Rational Expectations Hypothesis

The rational expectations hypothesis states that decision makers take into consideration all available information, including present and anticipated future economic policy changes, when forming their expectations about future economic variables, such as inflation.

According to this theory, expansionary monetary policy will cause wages to adjust upward in anticipation of higher inflation, almost immediately.

(*See also* Adaptive-Expectations Theory.)

## Say's Law

Say's Law proclaims that production generates its own demand. That is, the income generated from producing goods and services will always be available for purchasing them.

---

### Lesson from History

It is said that when Henry Ford started producing cars, he gave his employees generous paychecks so that they could afford to buy the cars they produced, thus creating their own demand for the cars.

---

## Supply-Side Economists

Supply-side economists believe that changes in marginal tax rates are critical to affect aggregate supply. These economists propose that marginal tax reductions will act as incentive for people to work more, save more, and invest more. This in itself will create more jobs and more efficient use of economic resources.

## Unemployment

### Frictional Unemployment

Frictional unemployment occurs because of the nonavailability, inaccurate nature, or high cost of obtaining information about job opportunities.

### Cyclical Unemployment

Unemployment caused by recessionary business conditions when there is inadequate aggregate demand for labor is known as cyclical unemployment.

### Natural Rate of Unemployment

The natural (normal) rate of unemployment includes unemployment arising from structural and frictional sources.

## Essay: Impact of Budget Deficit Reduction on Exchange Rate

The impact of budget deficits on the exchange rate of a country is a subject of much debate. Here's a summary of the findings of various studies on the subject.

In the short-term, the direct effect of budget deficit reduction makes the currency weaker.

Because of budget deficit reduction, government borrowing decreases; this reduces the interest rates, which makes domestic investments less attractive; therefore the demand for local currency will fall, leading to currency depreciation.

Hence, in the short term, a reduction in the budget deficit is likely to lead to depreciation in that country's currency.

In the long-term, deficit reduction indirectly causes the currency to appreciate, for three reasons:

- Increase in real rates of return
- Lower risk premium
- Higher return on domestic assets

A reduction in budget deficit decreases the need to print money. This causes inflation to decline, which in turn reduces the interest rate. But the decline in interest rate is not as much as the decline in inflation. Therefore, the effective real rate increases, making local investments attractive. The increased demand for the local currency causes an appreciation in the value of the currency.

Also, budget deficit reduction causes a reduction in government borrowing. This reduces the risk premium on local investments, which makes local bonds attractive. Again an increased demand for local currency causes that currency to appreciate.

Another indirect effect of budget deficit reduction is that it makes private sector investments attractive, since the government does not "crowd out" the private sector. These investments tend to increase private sector growth and productivity. Thus, domestic assets become more attractive, making the demand on local currency increase and its value appreciate.

The tax effect of deficit reduction also tends to cause an appreciation in the local currency, since after-tax return increases owing to a reduction in taxes.

### *Structural Unemployment*

Structural unemployment occurs because of the mismatch between job requirements and skills of unemployed workers.

## Velocity of Money

The velocity of money is the average number of times that a dollar is used to purchase goods and services during a year. It is given by:

Velocity of money = GDP/Stock of money

# SECTION 4

# Equities

## Beta

Beta is a measure of the *systematic risk* of a security. It measures the correlation of the returns on a security with the returns on the broad market.

Beta ranges from −1 to +1. A beta of −1 indicates that the stock is perfectly uncorrelated with the market; a beta of +1 indicates that the stock is perfectly correlated with the market.

Betas tend to regress toward the mean, over long periods. High beta portfolios tend to decline over time toward unity (1.0). Low beta portfolios tend to increase over time toward unity.

(*See also* Risks: Section 7.)

## Business Risk

Business risk is the uncertainty of cash flows caused by the nature of the business. It largely depends upon the volatility of earnings before interest and taxes (EBIT), which in turn is dependent upon the volatility of sales and the operating leverage of the firm.

## Business Valuation

There are three standard methods for valuing a business: fair market value, liquidation value, and going-concern value.

### Fair Market Value

Fair market value is the value that two rational individuals agree upon, based on all available information and without pressure or coercion.

Several computational methods are used to arrive at a fair market value. (*See* Dividend Discount Model; Price-Earnings Ratio.)

### Liquidation Value

Liquidation value is the value of a firm if all its assets were stripped and sold individually.

### Going-Concern Value

Going-concern value is the present value of all cash flows that the firm can generate in the future.

## Clientele Effect (Dividend Policy)

Different segments of the market invest in stocks with different levels of expectations on dividends. Thus, a certain segment of investors, such as retired people and widows or orphans, require a steady income from their investments and therefore invest in stocks that declare dividends regularly. To meet the expectations of these investors, companies declare dividends regularly even when it is not financially very appropriate to do so. On the other hand, companies that primarily attract wealthy individuals who are not in need of investment income may not declare dividends as often. This segmented approach is known as the clientele effect on the dividend policy of a company.

## Competitive Strategies (Michael Porter's Model)

According to Michael Porter's competitive model, there are five competitive forces that determine the success of a firm:

1. Threat of new competitors to the firm.

2. Threat of substitutes to the products of the firm.

3. Bargaining power of buyers (i.e., clients of the firm).

4. Bargaining power of suppliers to the firm.

5. Rivalry among competitors of the firm.

A firm can gain competitive advantage through two means:

- Low cost—the firm uses price as the key differentiator of its products.

- Product differentiation—the firm differentiates itself through its product features.

There are three generic competitive strategies that a firm can adopt:

- Cost leadership

- Product differentiation

- Focus (on niche markets)

## Dividend Discount Model

The dividend discount model (DDM) is a method for computing the fair price for any asset based on its expected dividend-paying capacity, growth rate, and discount rate. Two types of dividend discount models are described below.

### Constant Growth DDM

The constant growth DDM, used to price stock, is the simplest version of the dividend discount models.

**FORMULA**

$$P_0 = D_1/(k - g)$$

where

$P_0$ = Expected price of the stock

$D_1$ = Dividend expected in the next year

$k$ = Discount rate applicable to the stock

$g$ = Growth rate of dividends

**WEAKNESSES**

Despite its popularity, the constant growth DDM contains some weaknesses:

- It assumes that there will be no changes in any of its variables (dividend, payout ratio, earnings growth rate, and the discount factor) over the period of time.
- The model is inapplicable to companies paying little or no dividends ($D_1 = 0$).
- For companies with high growth rates, $g$ approaches $k$, and the model does not work for companies with growth rates greater than the discount rate ($g > k$).
- Risk is not explicitly defined in the model.
- Small changes in the growth rate ($g$) or the discount rate ($k$) can produce large variations in price.

### Variable Growth (Multistage) DDM

The variable growth model recognizes that the growth rate of companies varies depending on the stage of their life cycle, and deals with the different stages appropriately by using different values for each stage.

For instance, a two-stage DDM (also known as the *H model*) defines two stages: high growth and normal growth. A three-stage-DDM identifies three specific stages in a company's growth: high growth, deceleration, and maturity.

## Dividend Policy

The dividend policy of a firm determines the optimal amount of net income that should be distributed to shareholders as dividends after considering whether it is more profitable to plough back the profits in the business or to pay out profits to the shareholders.

There are different schools of thought on the optimum dividend policy. Theoretical models, such as the Modigliani-Miller theorem, state that dividend policy is irrelevant if no taxes are paid and the cost of raising capital is zero. However, practical considerations, such as the effects of taxes, flotation costs, and the clientele effect, do have an impact on the dividend policy.

In general, between value and growth firms the following will hold:

- Value firms should repurchase shares as their stock is undervalued.

- Growth firms should pay cash dividends as their stock is overvalued.

(*See also* Clientele Effect; Modigliani-Miller Propositions.)

## Dupont Model

The Dupont model provides a means of decomposing the return on equity (ROE) into five distinct components that help analysts understand how each major component of business affects the ROE of the firm.

The five components of ROE according to the Dupont model are:

1. Operating profit margin
2. Asset turnover
3. Financial leverage
4. Cost of debt
5. Tax retention rate

**FORMULAS**

The formulas for these components are based on sales, assets, earnings before taxes (EBT), and earnings before interest and taxes (EBIT).

Operating profit margin = EBIT/Sales

Asset turnover = Sales/Total assets

Financial leverage = Total assets/Shareholder equity

Cost of debt = EBT/EBIT

Tax retention rate = Net income/EBT

The above five components combine to affect ROE as follows:

ROE = (EBIT/Sales) · (Sales/Asset) · (Asset/Equity) · (EBT/EBIT) · (NI/EBT)

Several factors affect each of the components:

- Operating profit margin is affected by the competition, business cycle, and economic strategy.

- Asset turnover is affected by factors such as technology, productivity, efficiency, and the business cycle.

- Financial leverage is influenced by credit market conditions, management of the company, and industry characteristics.

- Cost of debt is affected by the amount of debt and the perceived riskiness of the company, which determines the interest rate on its debt.

- Tax retention rate is influenced by the level of taxes on the company's earnings.

## Earnings Multiplier Model

*See* Price-Earnings Ratio.

## Efficient Market Hypothesis

There are three forms of efficient markets as proposed by Eugene F. Fama in his landmark paper published in 1970.[1]

### Weak Form

The weak form of the efficient market hypothesis (EMH) states that all past data regarding a security are fully reflected in its current price. Therefore, such information is of no value to the investor and cannot be used to predict future prices.

This form of EMH negates the value of technical analysis.

### Semistrong Form

The semi-strong form of EMH states that all publicly available information has been quickly and efficiently reflected in the price of a security. Hence, such information is of no use in predicting changes in the price of securities.

[1]Eugene F. Fama, "Efficient Capital Markets: A Review of Theory and Empirical Work," *Journal of Finance,* vol. 25, no. 2 (May 1970).

The semistrong form of EMH challenges the usefulness of fundamental analysis.

### Strong Form

The strong form of EMH asserts that even nonpublic information (e.g., insider information) is not sufficient to consistently obtain extraordinary gains over time.

The strong form of EMH is an extreme view and is not consistent with U.S. securities market laws, theory, or practice.

## Engineered Investment Strategy

Engineered investment strategy (EIS) is based on a theory developed through quantitative analysis of past returns that projects a supposedly guaranteed performance of a security or portfolio. In order to be valid, EIS must be able to establish a sound reason for the past performance characteristic of the strategy and prove that such performance is repeatable in the future using the same strategy. It usually depends on highly quantitative models with complicated constructs.

EIS poses several potential problems and hence has not gained wide popularity. Some of these problems are:

- The rationale for past performance is insufficient and hence makes the model unreliable.

- Data mining—when any set of data is sufficiently manipulated, it can be made to reflect almost any theory that the analyst wants.

- The data used may suffer from certain biases. (*See* Look-Ahead Bias; Survivorship Bias.)

- Most statistical models assume a normal distribution of returns, whereas real-world data do not necessarily follow normal distribution.

## Equity Valuation Models

The formulas for eight basic models of equity valuation are given below.

### Price to Book Value

$P/BV$

where $P$ is the price of the security and $BV$ is the book value of the firm.

### Price to Replacement Value

$P/RC$

where $RC$ is the replacement cost.

### Liquidation Value

*See* Business Valuation.

### Net-Net Working Capital

Net working capital − Long-term debt

### Constant Dividend Model

$P_0 = D_1/r_p$

where

$P_0$ = Expected price

$D_1$ = Expected dividend for the next period

$r_p$ = Discount rate for the period

### Constant Growth Dividend Discount Model

$P_0 = D_1/(k - g)$

where

$P_0$ = Expected price

$D_1$ = Expected dividend for the next period

$k$ = Discount rate applicable to the security

$g$ = Expected growth rate of dividends

(*See* Dividend Discount Model for a detailed discussion.)

### Variable Growth Dividend Discount Model

$P_0 = D_1/(1 + k)^1 + D_2/(1 + k)^2 + \cdots + \{[D_n/(k - g)] \cdot [1/(1 + k)^n]\}$

where

$D_2$ = Expected dividend for the second period

$D_n$ = Expected dividend for the $n^{\text{th}}$ period

$n$ = Number of periods

### Earnings Model

$P_0/E = PR/(k - g)$

where

$PR = D_1/E$, (also known as the *payout ratio*)

$P_0$ = Price of the stock

$D_1$ = Dividend for the next period

$E$ = Earnings for the period

$k$ = Discount rate

$g$ = Growth rate of dividends

## Fourth Market

Direct trading of securities between two parties with no intermediary is referred to as the fourth market. Mostly, institutions with large positions may engage in such trades.

## Free Cash Flow

Free cash flow (FCF) is the total money available to investors after all investment opportunities available to the firm have been exhausted.

FCF can be expressed in two different ways: unlevered FCF and levered FCF.

### Unlevered FCF

For a firm that has no debt, the FCF can be expressed as follows:

$$\text{FCF} = \text{EBIT} \cdot (1 - t) + \text{Depreciation} + \text{Amortization} - \Delta\text{NWA} - \text{Capital Investments}$$

where

EBIT = Earnings before interest and taxes

NWA = Net working capital

$t$ = Tax rate applicable

### Levered FCF

For a firm that has debt in its capital structure, the FCF can be expressed as:

FCF = EBIT · $(1 - t)$ + Depreciation + Amortization –
ΔNWA – Capital investments – Preferred dividends –
Principal repayments + Proceeds from new debt issues

## Fundamental Analysis

Fundamental analysis uses extensive company, industry, and economic analysis to estimate fair market values for securities. Fundamental analysts believe that there is an intrinsic value for each security and that a proper analysis of all relevant data will reveal to the investor the fair market value of that security.

### Industry Life Cycle

Industry life cycle depicts the economic lifetime of an industry in five distinct stages. Almost all industries go through these five stages, perhaps to different degrees.

1. Initial or pioneering stage
2. Rapid or accelerated growth stage
3. Mature growth stage
4. Stabilization stage
5. Decline stage

Table 4-1 illustrates the characteristics of the five stages.

## Inflation

### Effect on Balance Sheet

Inflation affects the balance sheet in three distinct ways:

- When historical cost accounting is used, asset values are understated because of inflation.

## Table 4-1 Stages of the Industry Life Cycle

| Stage | Revenue | Profit Margin | Total Profits | Cash Flow |
|---|---|---|---|---|
| Pioneering | Low; high turnover ratio | Negative; low liquidity ratio | Negative; high debt/financial leverage ratio | Negative |
| Rapid growth | High; low turnover ratio | Very high; low ROA | High; High debt ratio | Low to negative |
| Mature growth | High; high turnover ratio | High; ROA normal | High; debt ratios normal | Negative |
| Stabilization | Stable; ratios normal | Decline | Stable | Highest |
| Decline | Decline | Squeezed | Decline | High |

ROA = return on assets.

- When the LIFO method of inventory accounting is used, inventory values are understated during high inflation periods.
- Liabilities in the balance sheet are, in general, overstated in a high inflation environment.

### Effect on Income Statement

Inflation tends have a significant impact on the income statement. Following are three direct effects of inflation on the income statement of a firm:

- Depreciation based on historical costs tends to overstate net income.
- Inventory valuations tend to be overstated.
- Net debtors tend to gain.

## Leading Indicators

Some of the other leading indicators of the economy are contracts and orders for plant and equipment, M2 money supply, change in trade inventories. The stock market is considered a leading indicator of the economy. However, the stock market is better at predicting economic recoveries than at predicting recessions. In the past, stock market performance has given seven false alarms about recessions (eight if we include the

1998 minicrash). The stock market decline, on average, precedes a recession by six months and precedes an economic recovery by about five months.

Hence, the stock market is considered a leading indicator of economic recovery.

## Look-Ahead Bias

Look-ahead bias occurs when an engineered investment strategy (EIS) is developed using data that are not normally available prior to the investment decision making.

Consider an investment strategy developed from P/E ratios that use annual EPS (earnings per share) figures as if it the data were available right at the end of each of year. In reality, these figures are not available to the investor until two months after the year-end. Because of this look-ahead bias, such an EIS will not yield the promised results.

(*See also* Engineered Investment Strategy.)

## Market Anomalies

Market anomalies are stock market outcomes that tend to repeat over time without a reasonable explanation. Four types of market anomalies are normally observed: value-based anomalies, earnings-based anomalies, price-based anomalies, and calendar-based anomalies.

### Value-Based Anomalies

Returns are inexplicably associated with the following variables:

- Low price-to-book ratio
- Low price-to-sales ratio
- Low price-to-cash-flow ratio
- Low price-earnings ratio
- Dividend yields when they are nil or very high

### Earnings-Based Anomalies

- Newly upgraded stocks tend to outperform the market (trends-in-analysts'-estimates effect).

- Stocks tend to outperform following a negative earnings surprise (earnings surprise effect).

- High-expectation stocks tend to have negative surprises; low-expectation stocks tend to have pleasant surprises (earnings torpedo effect).

- Late earnings reporters are often companies with bad news.

- Stocks with few analysts following them tend to outperform (neglected firm effect).

### Price-Based Anomalies

- Low-priced stocks tend to outperform high-priced stocks (price per share effect).

- Small cap stocks tend to have strong performance (market cap effect).

- Stock prices have a tendency to reverse course over long cycles as well as over the short run (price momentum effect).

- Stocks depressed near year-end are more likely to be sold for tax loss reason and then tend to bounce back in the new year (tax-loss-selling effect).

### Calendar-Based Anomalies

- Beginning and end of the trading day exhibit different returns and volatility behavior than midday (time-of-the-day effect).

- Start of the week tends to have poor performance but end of the week provides strong returns (day-of-the-week effect).

- Majority of return is earned during the first two weeks of the month (week-of-the-month effect).

- January returns are substantially different from the other months of the year (month-of-the-year effect or January effect).

Some of these anomalies challenge the conclusions of the semistrong and weak forms of efficient market theory. For instance, the earnings surprise effect and trends-in-analysts'-estimates effect challenge the semistrong form of market efficiency.

(*See also* Efficient Market Hypothesis.)

## Market Timing

Market timing strategists attempt to be invested in the market when it is rising and not to be invested (retaining earnings as cash) when it is falling. Research has proved market timing to be unprofitable over extended periods.

Three popular techniques used for market timing are:

- Technical analysis—studying stock price movements through charting and other methods.

- Valuation analysis—identifying periods when the market as a whole is relatively cheap, based on some valuation model.

- Economic forecasting—investing on the basis of the stock market cycle that is expected to precede the economic business cycle.

Market timing strategies are costly to implement and do not work in an efficient market.

## Minority Interest—Valuing

There are three general ways to value minority interest: top-down, horizontal, and bottom-up.

### Top-down Approach

The top-down approach involves three steps:

1. Estimate the enterprise value, using standard valuation method for valuing companies.

2. Compute the minority pro rata interest in the total firm.

3. Estimate applicable discounts.

### Horizontal Method

The horizontal method uses a direct comparison with sales of other minority interests in similar firms in similar markets.

### Bottom-up Approach

The bottom-up approach involves three steps:

1. Calculate projected cash flow of the company.
2. Estimate the amount realizable on the sale of interest.
3. Discount the amount to present value.

## Modigliani-Miller Propositions

Franco Modigliani and Merton Miller, two Nobel laureates, advanced two path-breaking propositions on a firm's capital structure.

### Proposition 1

Modigliani-Miller Proposition I states: "Assuming that there are no taxes paid, the value of a firm is independent of its capital structure." In other words, if a firm does not pay any taxes (i.e., $t = 0$), then free cash flow is independent of leverage.

We can see why this is true in Figure 4-1. Whichever way we cut the pie, the size of the pie itself remains the same.

### Proposition 2

Modigliani-Miller Proposition II states: "If taxes are taken into consideration, then a firm's capital structure with 100 percent debt is optimal." In other words, if a firm pays taxes (i.e., $t > 0$), then the greater the leverage and the higher the free cash flow; therefore, the higher the value of the firm.

### Figure 4–1   Modigliani-Miller Proposition I

Value of a firm not affected by capital structure

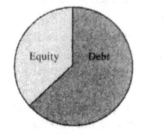
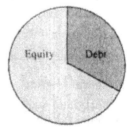

## Figure 4–2  Modigliani-Miller Proposition II

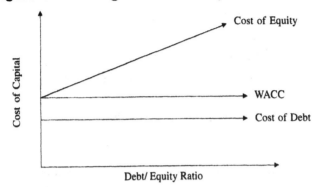

WACC = Weighted Average Cost of Capital

As can be seen in Figure 4-2, the cost of equity is a linear function and is dependent on the required rate of return on the firm's assets (also equal to the weighted average cost of capital, or WACC), the firm's cost of debt, and the firm's debt-equity ratio.

The above two propositions help us understand the issues when considering the optimal capital structure of a firm.

## Price-Earnings Ratio

The price-earnings ratio, or earnings multiplier, is a simple means of estimating the value of a firm based on its current market price and its expected earnings in the next year. In other words, it is a measure of how many dollars investors are willing to pay for a dollar of expected earnings in the next year.

### FORMULA

The P/E ratio is determined by the following formula:

$$P_1 / E_1 = (D_1/E_1) / (k - g)$$

where

$P_1$ = Price of the stock

$E_1$ = Earnings expected during the next year

$D_1/E_1$ = Dividend payout ratio

$D_1$ = Dividend expected during the following year

$k$ = Discount rate or the required rate of return on the stock

$g$ = Expected growth rate of dividends

## DETERMINANTS

The P/E ratio of a company is affected by the following eight factors:

1. EPS growth
2. EPS volatility
3. Extent of leverage
4. Market P/E
5. Average industry P/E
6. Prevailing interest rate
7. Speculation in the market
8. Quality of earnings

## USE

A high P/E ratio indicates high growth and/or low risk. High-growth companies typically pay low dividends, since they find it more profitable to plow back profits rather than distribute them as dividends. Hence, the stock price reflects this latent, undistributed value in the firm. Because of the low dividend and high price, these stocks typically have low dividend yields relative to the industry average.

Growth investors are primarily concerned with the earnings part of the P/E ratio. The growth investor believes that as earnings increase through growth, the price will increase correspondingly. However, the growth investor faces the risk of the anticipated growth not materializing.

Value investors, on the other hand, are primarily concerned with the price part of the P/E ratio. They are interested in under- or overpriced stocks. However, they face the risk of the stock being priced correctly by the market.

---

### Factoid About P/E Ratio

High variability of earnings is indicated by low P/E ratio.

Low growth rate of earnings is indicated by low P/E ratio.

Low debt (leverage) indicates low risk, hence high P/E ratio.

High inflation rate increases interest rates, leading to low P/E ratio.

---

## Random Walk Hypothesis

The random walk hypothesis is the forerunner of the efficient market hypothesis. According to this hypothesis, changes in stock prices occur randomly with no discernible pattern or rationale. There is a school of thought that still believes in the random walk hypothesis.

(*See also* Efficient Market Hypothesis.)

## Risk

*See* Risks: Section 7.

## Sector Rotation

Different sectors of the economy perform differently at each stage of the business cycle. Hence, selecting the appropriate sectors at each stage is one method of investing, which is called sector rotation.

See Figure 4-3. (*See also* Business Cycle: Section 3.)

### Capital Goods Stocks

Capital goods stocks are stocks of companies that are in the business of providing goods and services related to capital expenditure of a company. Stocks that belong to the following sectors are known as capital goods stocks:

## Figure 4–3 Sector Rotation and Business Cycle

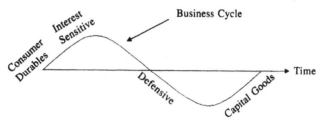

- Machinery
- Office equipment
- Computers

Investors tend to benefit from these stocks at the late stages of a business cycle, before the onset of a boom period, because significant investment in capital expenditure is likely to occur once the boom period commences.

### Consumer Durables Stocks

Consumer durables include items such as cars, washing machines, and televisions. Stocks that belong to the following sectors are known as consumer durables stocks:

- Automobiles
- Appliances
- Consumer electronics
- Department stores

Investors are likely to gain when they invest in these stocks around the midpoint in a business cycle.

### Defensive Stocks

Defensive stocks provide investors with protection against a decline in the business cycle. These stocks are expected to do well during a downturn in the business cycle.

Historically, stocks belonging to the following sectors have proved to be defensive stocks:

- Food
- Retailers

- Soft drinks
- Tobacco
- Drugs

It is appropriate for an investor to buy these stocks just prior to the end of a business cycle, before it enters a recessionary phase.

### Interest-Sensitive Stocks

Stocks that have a relatively greater sensitivity to changes in interest rates are known as interest-sensitive stocks. Investors seek to invest in these stocks just prior to the start of a boom period, when interest rates are expected to decline.

Stocks that belong to the following sectors are typically known to be sensitive to changes in interest rates:

- Public utilities
- Banking
- Insurance
- Finance
- Residential construction

These stocks perform poorly in the late stages of an expansion in the economy.

## Stock Dividends

When dividends are paid in the form of additional shares of stock, they are known as stock dividends. Since stock dividends increase the number of shares outstanding, the issue tends to dilute the value of each share.

## Stock Splits

Stock splits are essentially the same as stock dividends. Whereas stock dividends are expressed as a percentage of the face value of the stocks, stock splits are expressed as a ratio. In a stock split each share splits into multiple shares in a specified ratio. Stock splits also increase the number of outstanding shares and thus reduce the value per share.

## Survivorship Bias

If a research study does not take into consideration the fact that some of the data elements may have dropped out of the universe of data during the period under study, the research is reported to have survivorship bias.

For example, some companies may have gone out of business or delisted during the period of a study of stocks. If this fact is not taken into consideration, the study will be biased with the assumption that all companies that existed at the outset "survived" until the end of the study period.

## Technical Analysis

Technical analysis aims to predict stock prices by analyzing past price movements and volume information. It attempts to discern a pattern in price movements by charting prices over different periods in time.

Technical analysts believe that securities prices move in patterns, which repeat over long periods. Technical analysts develop trading rules from observation of the patterns, which they believe indicate buy or sell signals.

## Third Market

The over-the-counter market of shares and stocks is called the third market. (The first and second markets are the primary issue and the secondary trading on stock exchanges respectively.)

## Value Investing

Value investing is founded on the belief that at times certain stocks are mispriced (undervalued or overvalued) because of current news (bad or good). Once the news passes, these stocks will revert to their correct price, thus providing excess returns to value investors.

Value investors typically look for stocks with low P/E ratios or high yields. Value investors are considered to follow a contrarian strategy, since they usually buy when the market is declining and sell when the market is gaining, to take advantage of the mispricing of the stocks.

## Weighted Average Cost of Capital (WACC)

Weighted average cost of capital is the measure of the cost of capital of firm. It is calculated as follows:

$$\text{WACC} = (1 - t) \cdot r_d \cdot (V_D/V_A) + r_P \cdot (V_P/V_A) + r_{CE} \cdot (V_{CE}/V_A)$$

where

$t$ = Tax rate

$r_d$ = Interest rate on the debt

$V_D$ = Market value of the firm's total debt

$V_A$ = Market value of the firm's total assets

$r_P$ = Rate on the preference shares

$V_P$ = Market value of the preference shares

$r_{CE}$ = Rate on the common shares

$V_{CE}$ = Market value of the common equity

# SECTION 5

# Ethics

All concepts and terms in this section are defined according to the code of ethics and standards of professional conduct of the AIMR.[1]

## Affirmative Defense

In the event of a violation of a standard or law by an individual in an organization, the organization can claim in its defense if it can prove that it had put in place all necessary procedures and taken an affirmative action by enforcing precautionary measures to prevent such an event. Such a defense is termed an affirmative defense.

## Beneficial Ownership

A person is said to have a beneficial interest in a security if that person has:

[1]Association for Investment Management and Research.

- Direct or indirect pecuniary interest in the investment.
- The power to vote or direct the voting on the basis of ownership of the securities in the investment.
- The power to dispose or direct the disposition of the securities in the investment.

## Case Laws

For a background understanding on the case laws, *see* Material Nonpublic Information; Misappropriation Theory; Prudent Person Rule.

### Chiarella v. United States

This case established that the duty to disclose material, nonpublic information and/or abstain from trading on the basis of such information is applicable only if the person in possession of such information has a fiduciary duty to do so or should have known that such information was presented to him or her in breach of a fiduciary duty.

#### CASE FACTS

Chiarella was an employee of a financial printing press involved in printing materials relating to mergers and takeovers. In order to protect the identity of the takeover target all materials were printed with the takeover target left blank. Using the information available from the proof copies as well as library research, Chiarella deciphered who the takeover target was and invested in it. He was subsequently charged with trading on insider information. The court acquitted Chiarella, holding that he did not have a fiduciary duty to the takeover target, since he was not an agent of the company and since the counterparties to his trade did not place a duty of trust on him. The court also recognized the fact that Chiarella used a "mosaic concept" in putting together the valuable information.

### Dirks v. Securities and Exchange Commission

The U.S. Supreme Court's decision on this case extended fiduciary responsibility to "tippees," or persons who learn of material, nonpublic information. According to its ruling, a tippee inherits the fiduciary duty of an insider if (1) the insider breached a fiduciary duty in sharing the material nonpublic information and (2) the tippee knows or should have known that the insider disclosed the information in breach of his or her fiduciary duty. Also, the ruling reiterated that if the insider does not have any personal gain in disclosing the information, then the disclosure cannot be considered as a breach and the tippee may use the information.

**CASE FACTS**

Dirk, a securities analyst, obtained information from an ex-employee of a firm that the company was perpetrating massive fraud. Management denied the allegation. Nevertheless, Dirk disclosed the information to clients, who acted on it. The SEC found Dirk guilty of trading on material nonpublic information. However, the Supreme Court overturned the verdict in the ruling explained above.

### Harvard v. Amory

This landmark case in the Supreme Court of Massachusetts established the standard for fiduciary duty and prudence.

**CASE FACTS**

In its ruling, the court instructed that the fiduciary or trustee must "observe how men of prudence, discretion, and intelligence manage their own affairs, not in regard to speculation but in regard to the permanent disposition of their funds, considering their probable income as well as the probable safety of the capital to be invested."

This became the de facto definition for the prudent person rule.

### United States v. Carpenter

This case proved that the misappropriation theory can be applied to employees or persons not directly related to the issuer of a security, such as printers and journalists.

**CASE FACTS**

Some employees of the *Wall Street Journal* were convicted of insider trading. The author of the popular column "Heard on the Street" leaked information to others who benefited from material nonpublic information. These individuals had no direct fiduciary responsibility for the information they received. Nevertheless, they received such information in violation of the newspaper's policy of confidentiality of unpublished information. The employees were convicted of misappropriation.

### United States v. Chestman

This case illustrates another application of the misappropriation theory.

#### CASE FACTS

Kenneth Leob learned about an impending tender offer for the shares of Waldbaum's Supermarket from his wife, a member of the Waldbaum family.

The final judgment ruled that Leob did not owe a duty of confidentiality to the Waldbaum family, since he was not a confidant of their business affairs. Moreover, the court ruled that one party (in this case, the wife) cannot unilaterally impose a duty of confidentiality on another by merely sharing nonpublic information.

## Chinese Wall

*See* Fire Wall.

## ERISA

The Employee Retirement Income Security Act (ERISA) was enacted in the United States in 1974 to regulate all qualified private employee benefit plans in the United States. ERISA has acquired the reputation of being the de facto standard for prudence and fiduciary law, since several millions of dollars of pension plans are governed under this regulation.

## Fiduciary

A fiduciary is one who has been entrusted with the duty of caring for the assets of another person based on trust and confidence. A fiduciary is expected to act in the best interest of the person who entrusts his or her assets to the fiduciary. A higher degree of care and diligence is expected from the fiduciary than from an average person.

## Fiduciary Duties as Defined under ERISA

According to the U.S. Employee Retirement Income Security Act (ERISA), 1974, following are the duties of a fiduciary:

- The fiduciary should act solely in the interest of pension plan participants and beneficiaries.

- The fiduciary should perform duties for the exclusive purpose of providing benefits to plan participants and their beneficiaries, besides defraying reasonable plan administration and management expenses.

- The fiduciary should perform the functions with due care, skill, prudence, and diligence, under the circumstances then prevailing, in a manner that a prudent person acting in a like capacity and familiar with such matters would do in the conduct of an enterprise of a like character and with like aims. (*See* Prudent Expert Rule.)

- The fiduciary should diversify the investments of the plan such that the risk of large losses is minimized, except where such diversification is clearly not prudent under the circumstances.

- The fiduciary should always act in accordance with the governing plan documents, so long as they are consistent with ERISA.

## Fire Wall

Fire walls, also called Chinese walls, are physical and procedural barriers that prevent the flow of sensitive, material, nonpublic information between two or more departments within an organization.

For example, fire walls are put in place between the investment banking arm of a firm and its trading arm in order to prevent any sensitive information available to the investment banking group from reaching the trading section and thereby giving it an unfair advantage over other trading firms.

## Front Running

In the practice of front running, a trader or broker executes personal transactions or the organization's transactions ahead of his or her client's transaction to gain an unfair advantage over the client or the organization. Such an action is a violation of the code and standards of AIMR and securities law in many countries.

## Insider Information

*See* Material Nonpublic Information.

## Material Nonpublic Information

In the securities industry, information is "material" if the disclosure of that information is likely to have an impact on the price of a security or if it is likely to affect the decision of a reasonable investor in relation to the security.

Information is "nonpublic" if it is available only to a select group of people and not to the general public, and if general investors have not had an opportunity to act on it.

Trading based on material nonpublic information is known as *insider trading* and in the United States it is governed by the Insider Trading and Securities Fraud Enforcement Act (ISFEA).

## Misappropriation Theory

Under the misappropriation theory, any person who trades on the basis of material nonpublic information that has been misappropriated from another person can be found guilty of insider trading.

(*See also* Case Laws: United States v. Chestman.)

## Mosaic Theory

Mosaic theory states that an analyst will not be considered to have used material nonpublic information if he or she arrives at an investment recommendation or decision by using material public, nonmaterial public, and/or nonmaterial nonpublic information. Thus, even if such conclusions arrived at in the manner stated above would have been considered material nonpublic information had the analyst received it directly from the sources, the analyst would not be considered in violation of the law.

## Plagiarism

Plagiarism is defined as copying or reproducing, in substantially the same form, materials prepared by others without acknowledging the source or identifying the author or publisher of such material.

Plagiarism does not cover factual information published by recognized financial and statistical agencies or reporting services such as Standard & Poor or government statistical agencies.

## Prudent Expert Rule

The prudent expert rule is used to define the role of a fiduciary under ERISA.

A prudent expert must act with the care, skill, prudence, and diligence normally expected of an expert who is acting under similar circumstances then prevailing, and acting in a like capacity with familiarity of such matters as it relates to an enterprise of a like character and with like aims.

The distinguishing difference between this rule and common-law standard is that the rule is applied to the total portfolio rather than to individual investments within the portfolio.

The rule is also considered to carry a higher standard than the prudent man or prudent investor rule and is applied to fiduciaries managing investments under ERISA.

## Prudent Investor Rule

The prudent investor rule is the modern version of the prudent person rule and is founded on recent concepts in portfolio management such as modern portfolio theory. This rule recognizes the core consideration of portfolio management to be balancing the trade-off between risk and return.

Under the prudent investor rule, the fiduciary is expected to:

- Be loyal, impartial, and prudent in exercising the fiduciary duties.

- Make reasonable and suitable trade-offs between risk and return.

- Diversify the investments in the portfolio.

- Prudently select and delegate authority to experts and supervise them.

- Be cost-conscious in the management of the investments.

## Prudent Person Rule

Under the prudent person rule, the fiduciary has a duty to manage entrusted assets with the same care and discretion that a prudent person would employ to his or her own assets. This duty includes avoiding undue risk, preserving capital, and acting in the best interest of the beneficiaries of the investments.

## Soft Dollars

From time to time, an investment manager may benefit from research services purchased from brokerage commissions paid on customer transactions. This indirect payment using customer funds is known as soft dollars or soft commissions. Such soft-dollar arrangements are required to be disclosed to clients. Although soft dollars themselves are not illegal, some countries require that appropriate disclosures be made to the clients and that the benefits of such research information obtained ultimately benefit the clients.

## Tippee

A tippee is any person who learns material nonpublic information from an insider.

(*See also* Case Laws: Dirks v. SEC.)

## Tipper

A tipper is a person who conveys information to another person in violation of a confidence reposed in him or her or who breaches a duty of trust.

# SECTION 6

# Financial Statement Analysis

## Accounting Beta

Accounting beta measures the degree to which earnings of a firm vary relative to earnings of other firms in the economy.

Accounting beta can be expressed as the "total leverage effect" on the firm, which is defined as the product of the firm's operating leverage, financial leverage, and sales variance:

$$TLE = OLE \cdot FLE \cdot \text{Sales variance}$$

where

TLE = Total leverage effect

OLE = Operating leverage effect

FLE = Financial leverage effect

(*See also* Financial Leverage Effect; Operating Leverage Effect.)

## Accumulated Benefit Obligation (ABO)

*See* Pension Obligations.

## Accrual Accounting vs. Cash Accounting

Accrual accounting is the recognition of the economic reality of a transaction in the books of a company at the time that the legal transfers take place rather than when actual cash settlement occurs. Cash accounting, on the other hand, reflects the transaction in the books of accounts of a firm at the time of actual cash settlement.

Financial accounting standards require a firm to maintain its books of accounts on the basis of accrual accounting in order to reflect a true and fair view of the financial status of the firm.

Because of the difference in timing between when a transaction is recorded in the books of accounts and when the actual cash is received or paid for that transaction, the net income and cash flow of a company are not equivalent. Accrual accounting also introduces subjectivity as to when income or expense is recognized in the books and therefore calls for judgment on the part of the financial analyst to obtain a true picture of the state of affairs in a company.

## All-Current Method

*See* Foreign Currency Accounting.

## Book Value

Book value is the reported net worth of the company, and is usually expressed on a per share basis.

Book value per share = Common equity/ Shares outstanding

Book value primarily consists of:

- All capital raised from the shareholders in the form of common equity shares (less any shares repurchased).
- Retained earnings accumulated over the life of the firm.

- Any accounting adjustments that affect the shareholder equity section of the balance sheet.

A company can increase its book value per share either by buying back shares when the market price of its shares is below its book value or by issuing shares at a price above its book value per share.

## Cash Flow Statements

Cash flow statements are very important in enabling the financial analyst to get a true picture of the finances of a company. However, rather than rely on the cash flow statements provided by the firm, most prudent financial analysts construct their own financial statement using data provided elsewhere in the company's financial statements.

There are two methods constructing the cash flow statements—the direct method and the indirect method.

### Direct Method

Net sales

+/– Change in accounts receivable[1]

+ Other cash collections such as interest, dividends, etc.

= Cash collections/ receipts (**A**)

Cost of goods sold

+/– Change in inventory

+/– Change in accounts payable

= Cash inputs/ costs (**B**)

Cash expenses

+ Cash taxes

+ Cash interest paid

= Other cash outflows/ costs (**C**)

---

[1]An increase (decrease) in the accounts receivable from the previous period, as shown in the balance sheet, indicates a decrease (increase) in cash; hence subtract (add).

A – B – C = Cash flow from operations (CFO)

+ Change in plant and equipment

+ Change in marketable equity securities

= Cash flow from investing (CFI)

+ Change in debt (plus new issues, minus repayments)

+ Change in stock (plus new issues, minus repurchases)

– Dividends paid

= Cash flow from financing (CFF)

Net cash = CFO + CFI + CFF

### *Indirect Method*

Net Income

+ Noncash items (e.g., depreciation and amortization, plus accounts payable, minus accounts receivable)

+ Change in balance sheet items not yet affected (assets, liabilities)

= Cash flow from operations (CFO)

+ Change in plant and equipment

+ Change in marketable equity securities

= Cash flow from investing (CFI)

+ Change in debt (plus new issues, minus repayments)

+ Change in stock (plus new issues, minus repurchases)

– Dividends paid

= Cash flow from financing (CFF)

Net cash = CFO + CFI + CFF

## Company Valuation Models

Two popular models are used by financial analysts in valuing a company: asset-based models and discounted cash flow (DCF) models.

### Asset-Based Models

Asset-based models compute the value of a firm as the sum of the market values for the individual components of the firm, less the market value of the liabilities. This can be expressed as:

Value of firm = Market value of assets − Market value of liabilities

#### ADVANTAGES

- Asset-based models are useful to estimate minimum value.
- They are easy to use and understand.
- They are useful for comparing firms of similar size and nature.

#### DISADVANTAGES

- Book value in an asset-based model is based on historical cost.
- The firm's value is largely derived from its assets, whose value is dependent on management's choice of accounting principles.
- Asset-based models ignore future growth potential of the firm.

### Discounted Cash Flow (DCF) Models

Discounted cash flow (DCF) models value the firm on the basis of the present value of future cash flows that can be generated by the firm.

#### ADVANTAGES

- DCF models take into consideration future growth potential of the firm.
- The models are flexible enough to accommodate variable growth scenarios (using a variable growth dividend discount model).
- DCF models allow for scenario analysis that can highlight various possible outcomes.

**DISADVANTAGES**

- DCF models are sensitive to growth rate and discount rates assumptions (used in the dividend discount model).

- The models are not applicable when the growth rate exceeds the discount rate or when no dividends are paid.

- DCF models can suffer from measurement errors.

## Cost of Goods Sold (COGS)

Cost of goods sold (COGS) is an important factor in computing the net income of a firm. It is calculated using the following formula:

COGS = Purchases + Beginning inventory – Ending inventory

## Defensive Tactics

Companies adopt defensive tactics to defend themselves against hostile takeover bids. The most common defensive tactics are described below.

### Supermajority

Firms can use their corporate charter, which determines the rules of governance of the firm, to create high barriers to takeover. For example, a firm may have a provision in its charter that 80 percent of the shareholders on record should approve a merger proposal. This is called a supermajority provision.

### Repos/Standstill Agreement (Greenmail)

Firms coming under a takeover attack from an investor may negotiate a standstill agreement, whereby the investor agrees to limit holdings in the target company. In return the target company may agree to a "targeted repurchase" of some or all of the investor's holdings, usually at a substantial premium above the market price. This premium is sometimes referred to as *greenmail*.

### Exclusionary Self-Tender

In an exclusionary self-tender, the opposite of *targeted repurchase,* the target firm makes an attractive offer, usually well above the market price, to all shareholders excluding the unfriendly investor attempting a takeover. The practice may be viewed as discriminatory in the eyes of the law.

### Poison Pill (Poison Put)

In the fictionalized world of espionage, agents are trained to kill themselves by biting a poison pill to prevent the enemy from capturing them alive.

In the world of corporate finance, a poison pill consists of certain financial options that can be exercised by current shareholders to make it unattractive for a bidding firm to acquire the company. Typically these provisions include granting existing shareholders the right to purchase the shares of the company at a fixed price in the event of a takeover bid. The provision is intended to deter hostile takeover attempts.

A variation on the poison pill is the poison put, by which a firm is forced to buy back its shares at a specific price if it is taken over.

### Going Private

To avoid being taken over, a firm may decide to go private, taking its shares off the market and delist itself from stock exchanges. Thus takeovers through tender offers cannot occur, since there is no public listing of the shares.

### Golden Parachutes

Golden parachutes are special compensation provided to a firm's management in the event of a takeover. On the one hand, this additional cost is supposed to deter takeovers; on the other hand, it induces management not to resist takeovers that are in the best interest of the shareholders. Hence, golden parachutes provide a sweetener to get current management to step aside.

### Crown Jewels

A firm may sell or threaten to sell its major assets (its "crown jewels") when faced with a hostile takeover. This is also referred to as the *scorched-earth strategy.*

### White Knights

White knights are friendly firms that come to the rescue of a company threatened by a hostile takeover bid. The white knight might be invited to acquire large blocks of shares and effectively take over the company, thus thwarting the attempt of the hostile bidder.

### Lockups

A lockup is an option granted to a friendly firm giving it the right to purchase the stock of the company or some prime assets of the company at a fixed price in the event of a hostile takeover.

## Deferred Taxes

Deferred tax liability of a firm is defined as the total amount of taxes that will be paid in the future, under known tax laws, when the timing differences that have caused income reported for tax purposes to differ from income reported for book purposes is reversed.

The relationship can be expressed as follows:

Deferred tax liability (asset) for the period = Taxes that will be paid (tax credits that will be taken) when the timing difference is reversed.

Deferred taxes are important sources of distortion in financial statements. Hence, financial analysts must carefully examine the impact of deferred taxes, estimating when and to what extent such deferred liabilities are likely to hit the firm and assessing their impact on the firm's value.

## Defined Benefit Pension Plan

A defined benefit pension plan is one in which the plan sponsor (the employer) promises the employee a specified monetary benefit upon retirement. This benefit may be a fixed amount based on the number of years of service or an amount computed as the average salary drawn over a certain number of years of service, or variations thereof.

The essential characteristic of a defined benefit plan is that the employer bears the investment risk. That is, if the returns on the investments of the plan assets do not provide the expected return to cover the liabilities promised, the employer will have to provide for the gap.

## Defined Contribution Pension Plan

Under a defined contribution plan, the employer's liability is limited to contributing a fixed sum into the employee's pension plan every month. The performance of the investments in the plan does not affect the liability of the employer. Any variation in investment performance of the plan assets is borne by the employee. At the end of employment the employee is entitled to the total contributions made into the plan against his or her name. The employee can then purchase an annuity to provide for postemployment income.

The key characteristic of the defined contribution plan is that the risk of investment performance is carried by the employee.

## Depreciation

Five broad methods of computing depreciation are permitted under generally accepted accounting principles (GAAP) or U.S. tax laws. Generally Accepted Accounting Principles (GAAP) are accounting standards established by the Financial Accounting Standards Board (FASB). These standards govern the preparation of financial statements by companies in the United States. The Securities and Exchange Commission (SEC) requires that publicity traded companies comply with these standards and publish their accounts according to GAAP.

### Straight-Line Basis

Under the straight-line method an asset is depreciated over its useful life in equal installments after taking into account its salvage value. This method of depreciation is appropriate for assets that provide equal benefits throughout their useful life. The formula is given by:

Depreciation amount = (Asset cost – Salvage value)/
    Useful life

Suppose that an asset costing $100,000 has a useful life of 4 years and a salvage value of $20,000. The depreciation charged each year will be:

Depreciation amount = ($100,000 – $20,000)/4 years =
    $20,000

### Sum-of-the-Years'-Digits Depreciation

Sum-of-the-years'-digits depreciation is an accelerated depreciation method in which a higher proportion of the depreciation amount is charged in the early years and progressively lower amounts are charged in the following years. The method is based on the premise that the benefits accruing from the asset will decline as the years progress.

The method involves summing the digits of the asset's years of useful life and using the total as the denominator for fractional depreciation each year.

Suppose that an asset costing $100,000 has a useful life of 4 years and a salvage value of $20,000.

Sum of the years' digits = 1 + 2 + 3 + 4 = 10

In the first year the depreciation amount will be (4/10) · ($100,000 – $20,000) or $32,000. In the second year the depreciation amount will be (3/10) · ($100,000 – $20,000) or $24,000. And so forth.

In general, the depreciation amount is given by:

(Remaining # of years of useful life/ Sum of the years'
    digits) · (Asset cost – Salvage value)

### Double Declining Balance

Under the double declining balance method the depreciation amount is twice that of the straight-line method. The amount depreciated each year is declining at a faster rate as the fixed rate of depreciation is applied on a ever-decreasing asset value.

Hence, under this method the depreciation amount is computed as:

$(2/n) \cdot$ (Asset cost – Salvage value)

where $n$ is the number of years of useful life of the asset.

### Units of Production or Service Hours Methods

Under the units or service hours method, the depreciation amount is computed on the basis of actual units produced, or service hours provided, by the asset rather than on the passage of time. The depreciation amount is directly proportional to the usage of the asset. Thus, depreciation is high during periods of high usage of the asset, and vice versa. With this method depreciation becomes a variable cost rather than a fixed one.

### Combined Effect of Depreciation and Inventory Valuation

In a high inflationary environment the combination of straight-line depreciation and FIFO inventory valuation provides the highest reported earnings as compared with other combinations. (*See also* Inventory Valuation Methods.)

## Earnings Per Share (EPS)

### Basic EPS

The simplest form of earnings per share (EPS) can be expressed as follows:

EPS = Earnings available for common shareholders/
Weighted average number of common shares outstanding

The above formula can be used when the capital structure of the company is a simple one and does not include convertible securities that can potentially dilute the EPS.

#### CAPITAL STRUCTURE

Capital structure of a company refers to how a company has been financed using debt and equity capital. The capital structure of a firm influences its financial leverage and affects its debt-equity-ratio and other balance-sheet based ratios.

#### CONVERTIBLE SECURITIES

Convertible securities are usually securities such as bonds or preference shares that can be converted into equity shares in the company at predetermined price and/or time. They are attractive to investors who wish to retain the option of taking a stake in the company as a shareholder and participate in the upside of its stock prices. Companies that issue convertible securities find it useful to include the convertibility feature in order to reduce the cost of the debt by providing a sweetener to the investor.

### Primary EPS

Primary EPS takes into consideration the dilutive effect of convertible securities whose primary value is derived from their convertible feature. These securities are otherwise called common stock equivalents (CSE).

Primary EPS (PEPS) can be computed as follows:

PEPS = (Earnings available for common shareholders + Adjustments for CSE)/(Weighted average common shares + Weighted average CSE shares)

### Fully Diluted EPS

Fully diluted EPS (FDEPS) takes into consideration the impact of other potentially dilutive securities (OPDS). It is given by:

FDEPS = (Earnings available for common shareholders + Adjustments for CSE and OPDS)/(Weighted average common shares + Weighted average CSE and OPDS)

## Foreign Currency Accounting

There are two methods of accounting for operations when foreign currency is involved: the all-current method and the temporal method. Table 6-1 summarizes the required exchange rates under the two methods. Table 6-1 shows the appropriate exchange rate to be used for the various types of balance sheet and profit and loss accounts when converting the figures into another currency for reporting purposes.

### All-Current Method

When a subsidiary is integrated into the local economy and its decisions are predominately made at the local level, then the all-current method of foreign currency translation is used. In the all-current method the local currency is the functional currency and the focus is on *translating* foreign currency items into the reporting currency.

## Table 6-1 Exchange Rates in Foreign Currency Accounting

| Account | All-Current Method | Temporal Method |
| --- | --- | --- |
| Monetary assets | Current exchange rate | Current exchange rate |
| Inventory and prepaid expenses | Current exchange rate | Historical exchange rate |
| Plant assets | Current exchange rate | Historical exchange rate |
| Monetary liabilities | Current exchange rate | Current exchange rate |
| Nonmonetary liabilities | Current exchange rate | Historical exchange rate |
| Contributed capital | Historical exchange rate | Historical exchange rate |
| Retained earnings | No adjustments | No adjustments |
| Revenues | Actual exchange rate | Actual exchange rate |
| Cost of goods sold and depreciation | Actual exchange rate | Historical exchange rate |
| Other expenses | Actual exchange rate | Actual exchange rate |

### *Temporal Method*

When the head office (parent company) directs the operations of the local firm, the temporal method is used. Under the temporal method, the focus is on *remeasurement* of the foreign currency items into the reporting currency—the currency of the parent company. All monetary items are converted using the current rate of exchange, and nonmonetary items (such as inventory) are converted using historical rates.

Table 6-2 compares the two accounting methods. Table 6-2 gives a summary-at-a-glance of which foreign exchange rate to use for different elements of the financial statement under each of the two methods of foreign currency accounting.

## Functional Currency

Functional currency is the primary currency of the economic environment in which a firm operates. Functional currency is the local currency if a firm is fairly independent of its foreign parent such that most decisions are influenced by local environment and made by local management.

The local currency is not considered to be the functional currency if the parent exercises predominant influence on the local firm. Then the parent company's functional currency or any other currency designated by the parent becomes the functional currency of the firm.

Thus, functional currency may be different from the reporting currency, which is the currency in which the firm reports its financial statements to the parent.

If the functional currency is the local currency, then the All-Current method is used to account for foreign currency translation. If the functional currency is not the local currency, then the temporal method of accounting is used to account for foreign operations.

(*See* Foreign Currency Accounting for a description of the all-current and temporal methods.)

## Homemade Dividend

Under the homemade dividend concept, regardless of the dividend policy of a company, individual investors can create their own "dividend policy" by reinvesting dividends or selling shares of the company.

For instance, if the individual investor favors a no-dividend policy, preferring instead that the dividend payout be plowed back into the company, such an investor can achieve the same

## Table 6-2    Comparison of Accounting Methods

|  | All-Current Method | Temporal Method |
|---|---|---|
| Current rate | Balance sheet | Monetary assets and liabilities |
| Historical rate | Shareholder equity | Inventory; plant and equipment; shareholder equity; depreciation; cost of goods sold |
| Average rate | Income statement | Income statement |
| Translation adjustments | Shareholder equity | Income statement |

result by reinvesting any dividends in the stock of the company. Thus, instead of keeping the dividend, the investor helps increase the value of the stock. On the other hand, if an investor prefers to receive dividends and the company is not declaring any, the investor can sell some of his or her holdings and create cash. This will, in effect, reduce the value of the stock in the same manner as a dividend payout.

Thus, investors have the ability to create their own dividend policy.

## Intercorporate Investments

There are three methods for valuing intercorporate investments: cost method, equity method, and consolidation method.

### Cost Method

A company holding less than 20 percent of another company's share capital should treat it as marketable securities and account for that holding in its balance at cost. Any change in value to these investments must be reflected in the income statement and carried to the balance sheet through retained earnings.

### Equity Method

If a company holds between 20 percent and 50 percent of another company's share capital and if it is considered to have "significant influence" in the affairs of the company, then it should account for these holdings using the equity method. That is, any change in the value of these investments should be carried into the balance sheet through a change in value of shareholder equity.

### Consolidation Method

A company that holds more than 50 percent of another company's share capital and exercises control over that company should account for that holding using the consolidation method. Under this method, the holding company consolidates its balance sheet with the balance sheet of the company in which it has a majority, controlling interest.

(*See also* Marketable Equity Securities.)

## Internal Rate of Return (IRR)

Internal rate of return (IRR) is the discount rate that, when applied to a series of cash flows, equates the net present value (NPV) of the cash flows to zero.

In order for an investment to be considered good the IRR should be greater than the required rate of return for the investment.

(*See also* Net Present Value.)

## Inventory Valuation Methods

The method of valuing inventory has a significant impact on the income reported by the company as can be seen below:

### FIFO

In the first-in, first-out (FIFO) method of inventory valuation, the cost of the first item purchased is identified as the cost of the first item sold.

In an inflationary environment, this method of valuation will have a relatively low cost of goods sold; net income will therefore be overstated. Inventory values will be realistic, reflecting current replacement cost of the inventory.

### LIFO

In the last-in, first-out (LIFO) method of inventory valuation, the cost of the last item purchased is the cost attributed to the item sold.

In an inflationary environment, this method of valuation will have a high cost of goods sold; net income will therefore be understated. Similarly inventory will contain old, out-of-date cost; hence it is likely to be understated.

### Weighted Average

In the weighted average method, the weighted average cost of the items purchased is used as the cost of goods sold.

### Comparison of Methods

1. In a period of rising prices, earnings and inventory values will be lower under LIFO than under FIFO. In a period of falling prices, it will be vice versa.

2. FIFO tends to produce book value of inventories closer to market value than LIFO.

3. Under inflationary conditions, since FIFO tends to produce higher income and inventory values, it produces better financial ratios, which is good for obtaining credit arrangements. It also reflects well on the management.

4. LIFO tends to produce lower earnings and therefore higher after-tax cash flows relative to FIFO.

Table 6-3 summarizes the comparison.

### Combined Effect of Depreciation and Inventory Valuation

In a high inflationary environment, the combination of straight-line depreciation and FIFO inventory valuation provides the highest reported earnings as compared with other combinations.

(*See also* Depreciation.)

## Leases

### Capital or Financial Lease

A lease with *any one* of the following characteristics is a capital (financial) lease:

1. At the end of the lease, ownership of the lease property transfers to the lessee.

2. The lessee has the option to purchase the property at a bargain price at the end of the lease.

3. The period of the lease is 75 percent or more of the economic life of the property.

## Table 6-3   LIFO vs. FIFO

In an inflationary environment and when inventories are stable or increasing:

|                    | LIFO results in | FIFO results in |
|--------------------|-----------------|-----------------|
| Cost of goods sold | Higher          | Lower           |
| Net income         | Lower           | Higher          |
| Inventory values   | Lower           | Higher          |
| Taxes              | Lower           | Higher          |

4. The present value of the minimum lease payments equals or exceeds 90 percent of the fair value of the leased property.

Under a capital lease, interest payments are charged against cash flow from operations and principal payments are charged against cash flow from financing activities.

### Operating Lease

Leases that do not have any one of the four characteristics described above under capital or finance leases are known as operating leases. Under an operating lease, the full payment of principal and interest payments is included in cash flow from operations.

(*See also* Cash Flow Statements.)

## Leverage

Leverage indicates the extent to which a firm's income varies owing to variation in sales. A firm typically has two types of leverage: operating leverage and financial leverage.

### Operating Leverage

Operating leverage of a firm is the proportion of the firm's fixed costs relative to its variable costs. A high level of fixed costs indicates that the firm is highly leveraged and will have to have a consistently high demand in order to offset its fixed costs.

The operating leverage effect (OLE) on a firm can be expressed as:

OLE = Contribution / Operating income

OLE can be used as a measure to estimate the percentage change in income and return on assets for a given percentage change in sales volume.

### Financial Leverage

The proportion of fixed financing costs relative to share-holder equity is known as financial leverage. Financial leverage indicates the riskiness of a firm. A highly leveraged firm has a high fixed financing cost to meet before it can provide returns to its shareholders.

The financial leverage effect (FLE) on a firm can be expressed as:

FLE = Operating income/Net income

A high financial leverage when combined with a high operating leverage can be perilous to a company and can lead to financial distress in times of economic downturns.

### Total Leverage

The total leverage effect (TLE) of a company is the product of the operating leverage effect (OLE) and the financial leverage effect (FLE):

TLE = OLE · FLE

# Marketable Equity Securities, Accounting for (SFAS 115)

According to SFAS[1] 115, marketable equity securities can be classified under three broad categories for the purpose of accounting, depending on how the securities are held. Management has the discretion to classify securities under any of these categories.

### Securities Held for Trading

Securities identified as trading securities are marked to market. Any change in value of these securities is reflected in the income statement and carried to the balance sheet via retained earnings.

### Securities Held for Sale

Securities classified as held for sale are also marked to market. However, changes in the value of these securities are carried directly to the balance sheet, under shareholder equity, instead of posted to the income statement.

### Securities Held to Maturity

Securities classified as held to maturity are *not* marked to market. Changes in the value of these securities are not reflected

[1]Statement of Financial Accounting Standard.

in either the income statement or the balance sheet, unless such changes are due to a permanent impairment in value.

## Net Present Value (NPV)

Net present value (NPV) is the difference between an investment's market value and its cost.

For example, if the present value of an investment maturing in 3 years is $30,000, and the cost of investment is $25,000, it is said to have a positive net present value.

NPV is used to determine whether an investment should be made or rejected. The NPV of an investment should be positive in order for it to be accepted.

## Pension Obligations

According to accounting standards (FASB 87), companies must disclose the following three pension obligations in their financial statements.

### Projected Benefit Obligation (PBO)

Projected benefit obligation (PBO) is the pension obligation computed at a certain date, taking into consideration projected salary increases in the future.

### Accumulated Benefit Obligation (ABO)

Accumulated benefit obligation is the present value of all pension rights earned by the employees (vested as well as nonvested) up to today, based on current salaries.

It must be noted that ABO states only the accumulated obligation of a firm toward the pension benefits accrued over the past. It does not include future benefits that may be accumulated by the employees of a going concern. Hence, it typically understates the pension obligation of a firm. It is more useful in assessing the pension obligation of a firm that is about to be wound up.

### Vested Benefit Obligation (VBO)

Vested benefit obligation (VBO) is that part of the pension obligation of a firm that is not contingent upon future service.

This is the obligation that is owed to employees even if they cease employment at this time.

## Pooling Method of Acquisition

The pooling method of accounting for acquisition can be used under the following circumstances:

- The two companies (the acquiring and the acquired company) are independent companies.
- The acquisition is paid through the issue of voting common shares in the acquiring company.
- No stock repurchase is involved in the acquisition.
- There is no discrimination of shareholders.
- There are no disposal of assets immediately following the acquisition.

Here is an accounting checklist for a pooling method of acquisition:

1. Change the basis for depreciation by using fair market values for assets acquired.
2. Include additional interest expense (incurred because of debt issued for acquisition) in the income statement.
3. Include goodwill amortization. (Goodwill is the difference between the price paid and the fair market value.)
4. Take out tax.
5. Compute earnings per share (EPS).

Under the pooling method, EPS improves, and hence companies tend to show improved results immediately after acquisition, which could be deceptive.

Companies may prefer the purchase method over the pooling method of acquisition for the following reasons:

1. Price is less than book value.
2. Assets of the target company can be "written up" by using fair market value.
3. There is no dilution of interest of current shareholders in the acquiring company.

See Tables 6-4 and 6-5 for a comparison of the pooling and purchase methods of acquisition.

### Purchase Method of Acquisition

The accounting checklist for the purchase method of acquisition is as follows:

1. Use fair market value of "target" company (company being acquired).

2. Include goodwill in assets. (Goodwill is the difference between the price paid and the fair market value.)

3. Include new debt issued (to pay for the acquisition) in the balance sheet.

4. Include new equity issued (to pay for the acquisition) in shareholder equity.

5. Wipe out the "target" company's shareholder equity.

6. Check that the balance sheet balances.

The purchase method of accounting for acquisitions has two important effects:

- Adding goodwill to the asset base increases the net worth of the company. (It is somewhat ironic that under the purchase method of accounting, it is almost better to overpay for the acquisition, since this increases the net worth of the company.

- Earnings per share (EPS) declines because of (1) higher depreciation (since fair market value is used for the assets of the company) and (2) goodwill amortization, which affects net income.

See Tables 6-4 and 6-5 for a comparison of the purchase and pooling methods.

Companies may prefer the pooling method over the purchase method for the following reasons:

1. Price paid is greater than the book value.

2. There are no heavily depreciated assets in the target company (hence, no advantage in revaluing them).

3. There is no increase in leverage.

# Table 6-4   Comparison of Purchase and Pooling Methods

| Purchase | Pooling |
| --- | --- |

## BALANCE SHEET

| | |
| --- | --- |
| Recognizes fair market value of the assets of the company being acquired. | Does not recognize fair market value of assets. Assets are taken into the books of the acquiring firm at historical values. |

## INCOME STATEMENT

| | |
| --- | --- |
| Income statement of the acquiring company is restated from the date of acquisition forward. | Prior-period statements will have to be restated. |
| Cost of goods sold, depreciation, and goodwill amortization will be affected on the income statement. | No effect on any of these items. |

## CASH FLOW

| | |
| --- | --- |
| There is no change in cash flow from operations. However, cash flow from investments and cash flow from financing activities will change. | The cash flow statement is just the sum of the cash flows of the two companies. |

## RATIOS

| | |
| --- | --- |
| • Asset value ratios will increase because of restatement of assets to fair market value. | • Earnings-based ratios will be better than under the purchase method, since earnings are not affected by any goodwill amortization. |
| • Common equity-based ratios will increase as shareholder equity increases because of fair market value of assets. | • Profitability ratios will be better than under the purchase method. |
| • Earnings ratios will decline as a result of goodwill amortization and the subsequent decline in net income. For this reason income-based ratios (profitability ratios) will decline. | |

## TAX CONSIDERATIONS

| | |
| --- | --- |
| • Shareholders selling their shares to the purchasing company have to recognize the gain or loss on the sale (even if they are paid in the form of shares in the acquiring company). | • No gain or loss is recognized by the shareholders on the shares pooled. |
| • The tax basis for the assets and liabilities is changed to fair market value. | • Asset values remain at historical basis—hence the tax basis is not affected. |

## Table 6-5   Impact of Method of Acquisition on Financial Statements

| Line Item | Purchase | Pooling |
|---|---|---|
| Expenses | Higher | Lower |
| Net income | Lower | Higher |
| Assets | Higher | Lower |
| Liability | Higher | Lower |
| Equity | Higher (as assets are revalued) | Lower |
| Return on assets (net income/assets) | Lower | Higher |
| Return on Equity | Lower | Higher |

4. Fair market value exceeds historical costs of the assets being acquired.

(*See also* Pooling Method of Acquisition.)

## Projected Benefit Obligation (PBO)

*See* Pension Obligations.

## Ratios

### After-Tax Return on Assets

(Net income + (1 – Tax Rate) · (Interest expense))/ Average assets

### Current Ratio

The current ratio measures the ability of a firm to meet its current liabilities by liquidating its current assets.

Current assets/Current liabilities

### Debt-Equity Ratio

Total debt/Total equity

### Earnings per Share (EPS)

(Net income – Preferred dividend)/Average # of common shares outstanding

### Interest Coverage Ratio (Debt Service Ratio)

Earnings before interest and taxes/Interest

### Inventory Turnover Ratio

Cost of goods sold/Average inventory

### Leverage Ratio

Average assets/Average common equity

### Long-Term Debt–Capital Ratio

Long-term debt/(Long-term debt + Shareholder equity)

### Price-Earnings Ratio

Price per share/Earnings per share

### Profit Margin Ratio

Net income/sales

### Quick (Acid Test) Ratio

The quick ratio, also called the *acid test ratio,* measures how quickly the liquid assets of the company can be converted into cash to meet current liabilities.

(Current assets – Inventory)/Current liabilities

### Return on Common Shareholder Equity (ROE)

(Net income – Preferred dividend)/Average common equity

### Working Capital Turnover

Revenue/Average working capital

## Temporal Method

*See* Foreign Currency Accounting.

## Tobin's Q Ratio

The Q ratio, developed by Nobel Prize-winning economist James Tobin, measures the relationship between a company's market and book values. It is computed by dividing the market value of a firm by its book value on a replacement cost basis.

Tobin's Q Ratio = Market value of firm / Book value on replacement cost basis

Q values below 1 (market value less than replacement book value) imply that the firm's earnings are less than the required rate of return. Firms with low Q values are prime targets for takeover, since it is cheaper to buy these firms instead of building one.

## Vested Benefit Obligation (VBO)

*See* Pension Obligations.

## Z Score

The Z score is a number that is derived from a model developed by Edward I. Altman in his book, *Investing in Junk Bonds* (coauthored with Scott A. Nammacher, New York: John Wiley & Sons, 1987). It can be used to predict bankruptcy of a firm or to determine the credit risk of bonds, typically junk bonds. The model develops an overall credit score (zeta score) for a firm using traditional financial measures combined with a multivariate technique to derive a set of weights for the specified variables.

The model can be represented by:

$$\text{Zeta} = a_0 + a_1 X_1 + a_2 X_2 + a_3 X_3 \cdots + a_n X_n$$

where

$\text{Zeta}$ = Overall credit score

$X_1 \cdots X_n$ = Explanatory variables (ratios and market measures)

$A_0 \cdots a_n$ = Weightings or coefficients

The final model included the following seven financial variables:

$X_1$ = Profitability: Earnings before interest and taxes (EBIT)/Total assets (TA)

$X_2$ = Stability of profitability measure: the standard error of estimate of EBIT/TA

$X_3$ = Debt service capabilities: EBIT/Interest charges

$X_4$ = Cumulative profitability: Retained earnings/Total assets

$X_5$ = Liquidity: Current assets/Current liabilities

$X_6$ = Capitalization levels: Market value of equity/Total capital

$X_7$ = Size: total tangible assets

A Z score below 0 indicates that the firm is under distress and may default on its debt shortly.

# SECTION 7

# Fixed Income

## Active Fixed Income Portfolio Strategies

There are five recognized strategies for active fixed income portfolio management:

- Interest rate expectation strategies
- Yield curve strategies
- Yield spread strategy
- Individual security selection strategies
- OAS-based strategies

### Interest Rate Expectation Strategies

Interest rate expectation strategy exploits changes in the level of interest rates in managing the fixed income portfolio. This strategy can be effectively deployed by managing the duration of the portfolio or by swapping securities of different credit ratings.

In the first approach, the manager decides to increase or decrease the duration of the portfolio, depending on the direction of the movement of interest rates. If a parallel, downward shift in the yield curve is anticipated, then the manager could weight the portfolio such that it has longer duration, and vice versa. (Of course, the yield curve may not shift in a parallel fashion. In that case, the manager can use yield curve strategies discussed below).

In the second approach, the manager swaps bonds of different credit qualities to take advantage of movement in the price of these bonds. For instance, when interest rates rise, there is likely to be a flight to quality. Hence, Treasury securities will be more in demand. Therefore, if the manager is able to predict this increase in rates, he or she will swap some low-credit bonds for some high-quality ones.

### Yield Curve Strategies

Yield curve strategies aim to exploit anticipated changes in the shape of the yield curve (not just yield levels) by concentrating assets at specific points on the yield curve while maintaining the target duration.

There are three distinct yield curve strategies: bullet, barbell, and ladder. Each of these strategies will perform differently depending upon the type and magnitude of yield curve shift. See Figure 7-1.

### Figure 7–1 Bullet vs. Barbell

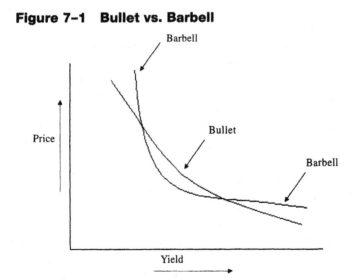

## BULLET

In a bullet strategy, the portfolio is composed in such a way that the maturities of the securities are concentrated at or near a single point in the yield curve—say, at 10 years' maturity.

See Figure 7-2.

## BARBELL

In a barbell strategy, the maturities of the securities in the portfolio are concentrated at two extreme points of the yield curve—say, at 5 and 20 years' maturity.

See Figure 7-3.

## LADDER

In the ladder strategy, the maturities of the securities are spread across the spectrum of the yield curve.

See Figure 7-4.

### Yield Spread Strategy

A yield spread strategy structures the portfolio so that the manager can capitalize on expected changes in yield spreads between different sectors of the bond market by shifting to the relatively undervalued sector.

## INTERMARKET SWAP

Bonds of different credit quality perform differently depending upon the state of the business cycle and the corresponding level of interest rates. During an economic decline, bonds of good credit quality are in demand, and vice versa. In general, the spread between Treasury securities and non-Treasury securities tends to widen during recessions and narrow during expansions. Hence, a bond portfolio manager who anticipates a decline in the economy will swap low-credit bonds for Treasury securities or high-quality bonds. This is also called *flight to quality.*

A similar swap strategy may be deployed during declining or increasing interest rate scenarios.

Swaps can also be used to move between callable and non-callable bonds, which may perform differently depending on the direction and pace of movement in interest rates.

**Figure 7-2  Bullet Strategy**

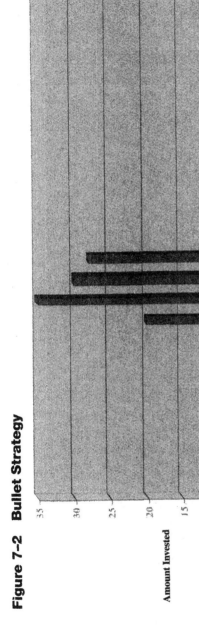

**Figure 7–3** **Barbell Strategy**

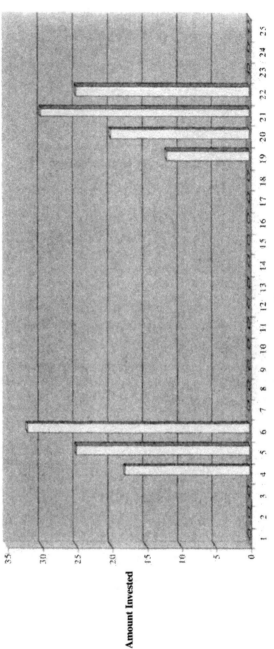

Amount Invested

Years

Figure 7-4  Ladder Strategy

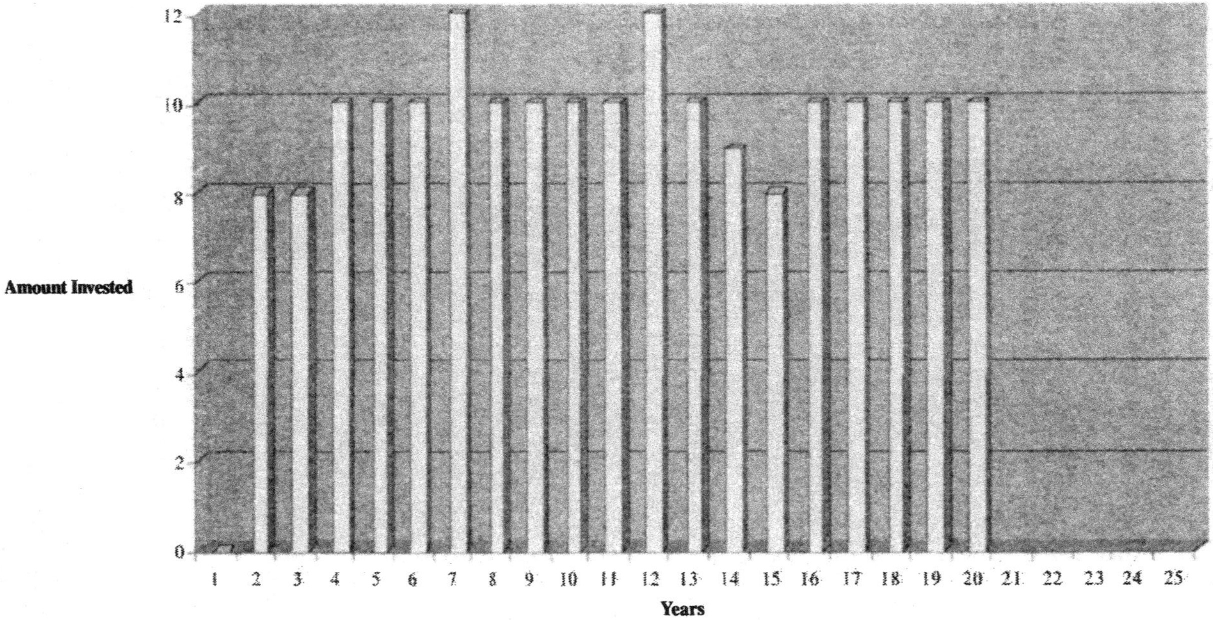

### Individual Security Selection Strategies

Individual security selection strategies exploit returns generated from repricing of bonds by investing in mispriced securities.

#### SUBSTITUTION SWAP

In a substitution swap, a bond is swapped with another one that has identical coupon rate, maturity, and credit quality but offers a higher yield to maturity.

### OAS-Based Strategies

Strategies based on the option-adjusted spread (OAS) aim to exploit the changes in the price of options embedded in fixed income securities by changing the exposure to these option features.

### Summary of Fixed Income Strategies

Here is when to use which strategy:

- For changes in the level of interest rates—use interest rate anticipation strategies.

- For changes in the shape of the yield curve—use duration-neutral yield curve strategies.

- For changes in yield spreads between different sectors—use yield spread strategies.

- For changes in the yield spread for a particular instrument—use individual security yield spread strategies.

## Average Life

Average life is a measure of the weighted average time to the return of a dollar of principal. It is similar to *duration,* except that duration considers the timing of total cash flow, whereas average life considers only the receipt of the principal component.

Average life is commonly used in measuring the investment life of Mortgage-backed securities. Here is an example of calculating the average life of a bond with balloon payments:

| Time (year) | Principal Repayment ($) | Time · Principal |
|---|---|---|
| 1 | 0 | 0 |
| 2 | 10 | 10 |
| 3 | 20 | 60 |
| 4 | 30 | 120 |
| Total | 60 | 190 |

Average life = Sum of (Time · Principal)/Total principal

Average life = 190/60 = 3 years, 2 months

(*See also* Duration; Mortgage Pass-Through Securities.)

## Barbell and Bullet

*See* Active Fixed Income Portfolio Strategies: Yield Curve Strategies.

## Bond Indexes

Two bond indexes are popular among bond portfolio managers:

- Lehman Government Corporate Bond Index
- Lehman Aggregate Bond Index

These indexes are used as benchmarks to compare the performances of bond managers. Hence, bond managers have to understand the composition and characteristics of these indexes in order to beat them.

### Lehman Government Corporate Bond Index

The Lehman Government Corporate Bond Index is primarily composed of U.S. government, agency, and corporate securities. The index composition represents the relative distribution of these securities in the fixed income market, with the exclusion of the mortgage market. Nearly three-fourths of the index is composed of government and agency securities.

### Lehman Aggregate Bond Index

The Lehman Aggregate Bond Index is similar to the Lehman Government Corporate Bond Index; except that mortgages are included in the aggregate index. Because of the inclusion of mortgages, the character and performance of this index differ significantly from the government/corporate index.

(*See also* Indexing Strategies.)

## Bootstrapping

Bootstrapping is the process by which two spot rates for different periods are used to compute the expected future spot rate for a corresponding (or intermediate period).

For instance, if you have the six-month spot rate and the one-year spot rate, then the expected six-month spot rate that will be applicable six months from today can be computed using the two spot rates. The formula is expressed as follows:

Price = $C_1/(1 + r_1)^1 + (C_2 + P)/(1 + r_2)^2$

where

$C_1$ = First coupon interest

$C_2$ = Second coupon interest

$P$ = Principal amount

$r_1$ = Spot rate applicable to discount the first coupon

$r_2$ = Spot rate applicable to discount the second coupon

Assume that the current six-month semiannual spot rate is 5 percent and that a one-year bond with two coupon payments of $30 each is priced at $950. Thus:

$950 = 30/(1 + 0.05) + (30 + 1000)/(1 + r_2)^2$

Solving for $r_2$, we get 0.0573 or 5.73 percent. When this figure is annualized, we get 11.46 percent as the spot rate that is applicable for the second 6-month period. In other words, 11.46 percent is the spot rate that will prevail six months from now.

(*See also* Spot Rate.)

## Callable Bonds—Price-Yield Relationship

Bonds that have a call feature embedded in them are referred to as callable bonds. Callable bonds exhibit different price characteristics from noncallable bonds, as shown in Figure 7-5.

## Figure 7–5    Callable Bond vs. Noncallable Bond

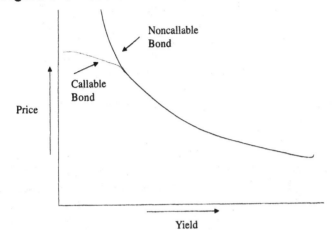

The price of a callable bond can be expressed as follows:

Price of a callable bond = Price of a noncallable bond – Price of the call option

For the issuer of a bond, the embedded call option in a callable bond is:

- In the money when the market interest rate is less than the coupon rate.

- At the money when the market interest rate is equal to the coupon rate.

- Out of the money when the market interest rate is greater than the coupon rate.

(*See also* Options: Section 2.)

## Call Risk

*See* Risks.

## Collateralized Mortgage Obligations (CMOs)

Collateralized mortgage obligations (CMOs) are derivatives that help to redistribute interest rate and prepayment risks inherent in mortgages.

In practice, CMOs are sliced into different series, or tranches, with each tranche having its own collateral of interest or principal payments. In a "plain vanilla CMO," all tranches except the first are backed by interest payments. The first one is backed by principal payments. Once the first tranche is paid off, the subsequent principal repayments are used to prepay the remaining tranches in sequence.

There are several variations of the CMO structure.

### IOs

Interest-only securities (IOs) are CMO structures in which all the interest payments on a collection of mortgages is packaged and sold as a tranche. These securities are also sold at a deep discount to their notional principal amount.

At high prepayment rates, investors could receive less cash flow over the life of the security. IOs thus have negative convexity: Because of declining interest rates, IOs decline in value as prepayments increase. (*See* Convexity.)

In conclusion, faster prepayment rate is not good for an IO tranche.

### Jump Zs

A Jump Z tranche is one that "jumps" the queue and receives payments ahead of the other tranches because of some pre-specified trigger event.

### PACs

Planned amortization classes (PACs) are tranches that are amortized using a sinking-fund schedule. Each PAC has a companion tranche that absorbs unexpected prepayments, thus protecting the PAC from uncertainty of cash flows. As a result, PACs have fairly high predictability and are more suited for investors who prefer certainty of cash flow.

### POs

Principal-only securities (POs) are CMO structures that are stripped off the coupon interest and sold at a deep discount to face value.

These securities are extremely sensitive to prepayment rates. During periods of interest rate decline, prepayments will increase and the PO tranche may receive higher and earlier prepayments, resulting in higher yield. Hence, POs have positive convexity. (*See* Convexity.)

In sum, an increase in prepayment rates is good for a PO tranche.

### TACs

Targeted amortization classes (TACs) are similar to PACs in that they have a reasonably predictable cash flow using a sinking-fund schedule. However, unlike PACs, they are not protected against *both* faster and slower prepayments.

TACs are suitable for investors who want some cash flow predictability but are sure about the direction of movement in interest rates, which cause changes in prepayment rates.

### VADMs

Very accurately defined maturities (VADMs) are tranches that have a highly structured cash flow pattern in which principal repayments are accumulated and reinvested to create a predictable maturity schedule.

### Z Tranche

A Z tranche is the last tranche that is paid off in a CMO structure. Z tranches receive no interest or principal payments until all other tranches have been paid off. A Z tranche also acts as a stabilizer, since the interest from it is used to pay off other tranches, thus stabilizing their prepayments.

## Contraction Risk

*See* Risks.

## Convexity

Convexity measures the rate of change of duration as yields change.

### Convexity vs. Duration

Although duration is a good measure of the percentage price change for small changes in yield, for large changes in yield, duration alone is unable to explain the extent of the price change. As can be seen in Figure 7-6, at extreme ends of yield levels the curvature of the price-yield curve is significant and hence duration is a poor approximation at these levels. Here, convexity provides the additional information of the extent of price change that can be expected at these levels of yield changes.

Convexity can also be seen as a measure of the rate of change of duration as yields change. The formula is as follows:

Convexity (in years) = $[n^2 \cdot (CF_i) / (1 + y/2)^n]/4 \cdot$ Price

where

$n$ = Number of periods

$CF_i$ = Cash flow in period $i$

$y$ = Yield on the bond

Modified convexity = Convexity/$(1 + y/2)^2$

Percentage change in price of bond = ½ · Modified convexity · $(\Delta y)^2 \cdot (100)^2$

where $\Delta y$ is the change in yield.

### Figure 7–6   Convexity

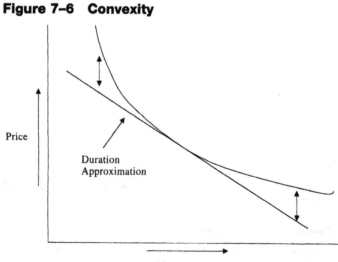

Price

Duration Approximation

Yield

Convexity gains importance when market interest rates are high or when there is large variation in market interest rates.

### Positive vs. Negative Convexity

Positive convexity implies that the bond price will increase at a faster rate when yields drop than they decrease when the yields rise.

---

### Factoids About Convexity

Holding coupon and maturity constant, the higher the yield, the lower the duration and convexity.

Holding yield and maturity constant, the higher the coupon, the lower the duration and convexity.

All other things being equal, investors prefer to hold bonds with greater convexity.

---

For a bond that has an embedded call option, when market interest rates fall below the coupon rate, there is a likelihood of the bond being called. Therefore the price of the bond ceases to appreciate. Instead, as the yield drops, the price drops even further. This reversal of price appreciation with a drop in yield due to the call feature produces a negative convexity on the bond.

Bonds that have a call feature exhibit negative convexity when market interest rates are low, as shown in Figure 7-7. However, they display positive convexity when market interest rates are high, since there is less likelihood of the bond being called.

## Constant Prepayment Rate (CPR)

Constant prepayment rate is a measure of the extent of prepayments that might occur on a pool of mortgages because of a decline in interest rates. It is expressed as a percentage of the outstanding mortgages that might terminate from prepayment during a period, usually one year. CPR is usually expressed on an annualized basis. It is based on monthly pre-

## Figure 7–7    Negative Convexity

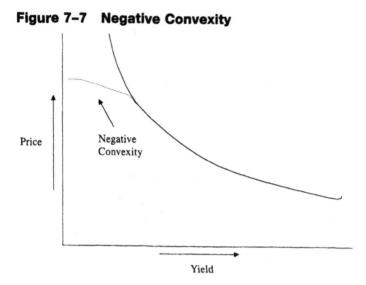

payment calculations, which are called *single monthly mortality* (SMM). When these are compounded within the year, it is called a *constant monthly prepayment* (CMP).

### Credit Enhancements

*See* Credit Quality Enhancement.

### Credit Quality Enhancement

Credit quality enhancements help improve the credit on a bond or an asset-backed security, thereby reducing the risk premium on the issue.

Some of the credit enhancement techniques include:

- Creating a reserve fund or a sinking fund that will guarantee the repayment of the principal.
- Obtaining third-party guarantees (e.g., from parent company, government, or bank) of higher credit quality.
- Providing cash collaterals that offer protection in the event of default.

## Credit Ratings

When a country or company wishes to issue debt instruments in the market, it will seek to obtain a rating for the issue. This is referred to as credit rating or bond rating.

Credit ratings attempt to determine the creditworthiness of the issuers of the bond and their ability to repay the principal and interest in a timely manner. Several quantitative and qualitative factors are considered in determining the rating.

Table 7-1 lists some of the ratings used by the two popular credit rating agencies, Moody's and Standard & Poor's.

Issues that have a rating of BBB or better are classified as investment-grade bonds. Issues that carry a rating of BB and below are considered speculative.

Table 7-2 is based on a three-year median of ratios normally used by rating agencies such as Standard & Poor's. It must be noted, however, that industry financial ratios can change over time and for different industries.

## Credit Risk

*See* Risks.

## Current Yield

Current yield is the annual coupon payment on a bond relative to the prevailing market price of the bond.

Current yield = Coupon interest/Market price

Current yield is a useful measure for investors who buy bonds for the income component rather than the total return (i.e., capital gains included). It is similar to the dividend yield on a stock.

## Duration

Duration is the weighted average time to maturity of a bond. In fixed income portfolios it is useful as:

# Table 7-1   Types of Credit Ratings

| S&P | Moody's | Description of Rating |
|-----|---------|----------------------|

### HIGH GRADE

| S&P | Moody's | Description of Rating |
|-----|---------|----------------------|
| AAA | Aaa | Bonds of this highest rating, also called *gilt-edge securities*, have an extremely strong capacity to pay principal and interest in a timely manner. |
| AA | Aa | These high-quality bonds have a strong capacity to pay principal and interest in a timely manner. They are marginally less protective than AAA bonds. |

### MEDIUM GRADE

| S&P | Moody's | Description of Rating |
|-----|---------|----------------------|
| A | A | Medium-grade bonds have the capacity to repay principal and interest in a timely manner, but have elements that suggest susceptibility to adverse economic changes. |
| BBB | Baa | These bonds currently have the ability to pay principal and interest but do not have adequate protection in the event of a business or economic downturn that may make the issuer unable service the debt. |

### SPECULATIVE GRADE

| S&P | Moody's | Description of Rating |
|-----|---------|----------------------|
| BB | Ba | Speculative-grade bonds offer only moderate protection of principal and interest payments and may be adversely affected during good as well as bad economic conditions. |
| B | B | These bonds have only a moderate assurance of principal and interest repayments on a timely basis. |

### DEFAULT

| S&P | Moody's | Description of Rating |
|-----|---------|----------------------|
| CCC | Caa | A default rating indicates that the issue is susceptible to default if current economic and business conditions continue to prevail. |
| CC | Ca | Bonds with this rating are highly speculative and are often in default or in imminent danger of default. |
| C | | This rating is given to income bonds on which no interest is being paid—that is, bonds that are currently not being serviced. |
| D | | This rating means that the issue is in default and principal and interest payments are in arrears. |

### SPECIAL NOTATION

| S&P | Moody's | Description of Rating |
|-----|---------|----------------------|
| r | | This symbol indicates that the issue may carry non-credit-related risks, such as prepayment risk carried by a mortgaged-backed security. |
| + or − | | A + or − sign may be used in conjunction with the above ratings to provide subclassifications within each rating. |

### Table 7-2   Key Industrial Financial Ratios

| Ratio | AAA | A | BB |
|---|---|---|---|
| Pretax interest coverage (times) | 16.66 | 4.63 | 1.59 |
| Pretax fixed-charge coverage including rents (times) | 6.34 | 2.93 | 1.33 |
| Pretax funds flow interest coverage (times) | 22.99 | 7.21 | 2.75 |
| Funds from operations/Total debt (%) | 134.7 | 44.4 | 17.9 |
| Free operating cash flow/Total debt (%) | 49.2 | 17.0 | 0.9 |
| Pretax return on permanent capital (%) | 24.2 | 13.5 | 9.1 |
| Operating income/Sales (%) | 22.5 | 13.8 | 10.6 |
| Long-term debt/Capitalization (%) | 11.7 | 29.4 | 51.1 |
| Total debt/Capitalization (%) | 23.2 | 36.7 | 56.3 |

- A measure of average maturity
- A tool in immunizing the portfolio from interest rate risk (*see* Immunization Strategies)
- A measure of interest rate sensitivity

Duration comes in two forms: Macaulay duration and modified duration.

Macaulay duration: $\sum (t) \cdot$ (Present value of cash flows)/ Bond price

Modified duration: (Macaulay duration)/$(1 + r)$

where $t$ is time and $r$ is the interest rate.

---

### Factoid About Duration

The duration of a zero coupon bond equals its time to maturity.

Holding maturity constant, a bond's duration is higher when the coupon rate is higher.

Holding coupon rate constant, a bond's duration generally increases with its time to maturity.

### Effective Duration

Effective duration or option-adjusted duration measures the responsiveness of bond prices to changes in interest rates after taking into account the fact that the cash flow expected from a bond could change because of its embedded option.

In other words, whereas modified duration assumes that yield changes do not change expected cash flows, effective duration considers cash flow changes based on yield changes owing to embedded call features in a bond.

The formula is given as:

Effective duration = $(P_- - P_+)/2\,P_0(\Delta y)$

where

   $P_-$ = Price of the bond if yield decreases by $x$ basis points

   $P_+$ = Price of the bond if yield increases by $x$ basis points

   $P_0$ = Initial price (per $100 of par value)

   $\Delta y$ = Change in yield used to calculate the price ($x$ basis points in decimal form)

(*See also* Duration.)

### Partial Duration

Partial duration quantifies the risk of a nonparallel shift in yield curve. It can be computed by defining the key interest rate and determining the percentage price change for a change of 100 basis points in the key interest rate, when other rates are held constant.

Partial duration provides information on how changes in the shape of the yield curve affect the value of the portfolio. It is especially useful when mortgage-backed securities in a portfolio are sensitive to yield curve changes. (*See also* Duration.)

## Double-Barreled Bond

A double-barreled bond is a municipal bond that is backed by the general taxing power of the municipality as well as by other municipal revenues.

## Effective Annual Yield

Effective annual yield is the annualized yield computed as follows:

Effective annual yield = $(1 + r)^n - 1$

where $r$ is the periodic interest rate and $n$ is the number of periods.

For example, if the semiannual interest rate is 3.8 percent, the effective annual yield is $(1.038)^2 - 1 = 7.74$ percent.

## Effective Convexity

Effective convexity is the convexity measure that takes into consideration the impact of the embedded option on the price movements of the bond. It is represented by:

Effective convexity = $(P_- + P_+ - 2 P_0)/(P_0 (\Delta y)^2$

where

$P_-$ = Price of the bond if yield decreases by $x$ basis points

$P_+$ = Price of the bond if yield increases by $x$ basis points

$P_0$ = Initial price (per $100 of par value)

$\Delta y$ = Change in yield used to calculate the price ($x$ basis points in decimal form)

When a bond has an embedded option, it is more appropriate to use this formula to compute convexity.

(*See also* Convexity.)

## Eurobonds

Eurobonds are bonds denominated in U.S. dollars that are traded outside the issuing country. These instruments are largely used to issue sovereign debt, and a syndicate of international investment banking houses usually underwrites them. They are issued in bearer form.

## Exchange Variable Rate Notes (EVRNs)

Exchange variable rate notes (EVRNs) are subordinated, intermediate-term notes that pay quarterly interest. Typically,

EVRNs carry a high initial fixed rate, which converts into a floating rate according to a benchmark such as 90-day U.S. Treasury bills.

The issuer of EVRNs usually retains the option to exchange them for fixed rate notes with predetermined features.

EVRNs are useful fixed income instruments for a company that wishes to attract investors initially but wants to retain the option to convert to floating rate once it has established a good credit history. At that time, investors may choose to retain the instrument because of improved credit.

## Expectations Hypothesis

*See* Term Structure of Interest Rates.

## Extension Risk

*See* Risks.

## Forward Rate

A forward rate is the interest rate for a loan between any two dates in the future, contracted today. For example, the one-year rate expected to prevail three years from now may be 8 percent.

The forward rate is purely based on expectation, which is in turn based on prevailing bond prices—which are of course subject to constant change. Forward rates help investors assess the market expectation on future interest rates.

## Forward Rate Agreements

Forward rate agreements (FRAs) are over-the-counter contracts entered into by two parties for the future purchase or sale of a specific interest.

## High-Yield Credit Analysis

High-yield bonds require special credit analysis that should cover the following areas:

- Level and type of competition
- Dependability of cash flow
- Size of net assets
- Quality of management
- Extent of leverage in the balance sheet

## Horizon Return

*See* Horizon Yield.

## Horizon Yield

Horizon yield, also called *realized yield,* is the rate of return expected on a bond if the bond were to be sold prior to its maturity. It is a useful measure of bond returns, since bonds are often sold prior to maturity.

An approximate realized yield can be computed using the formula:

$$\text{Approximate realized yield} = \frac{CPN + [(P_s - P_m)/n_h]}{(P_s + P_m)/2}$$

where

$CPN$ = Coupon on the bond

$P_s$ = Expected sale price of the bond

$P_m$ = Market price of the bond

$n_h$ = Expected holding period of the bond

## Indexes

*See* Bond Indexes.

## Indexing Strategies

Indexing is a strategy that attempts to replicate the performance of a market index such as the Lehman Aggregate Bond Index or Lehman Government Corporate Bond Index.

Indexing provides several advantages to the investor:

- Low risk of underperforming the market (represented by the index).

- Less dependence on interest rate forecasts, which are unpredictable.

- Reduced investment advisory fees and custodial fees.

- Greater control over the investment manager's actions on the portfolio.

- Greater objectivity in evaluating the performance of the investment manager.

There are five alternate methods for indexing a fixed income portfolio:

1. Enhanced indexing

2. Full replication

3. Stratified sampling or cell approach

4. Optimization approaches

5. Variance minimization approach

(*See also* Bond Indexes.)

### Enhanced Indexing

Enhanced indexing is a strategy adopted by some index fund managers. Under this strategy, the index fund manager selectively deviates from the index to take advantage of specific investment opportunities by deploying additional techniques such as sector selection and yield curve strategies.

The more a manager deviates from the index, the greater the potential for enhanced return and the greater the risk of underperforming the index.

### Full Replication

Full replication involves constructing a portfolio by purchasing each security in the index at the appropriate market weighting.

#### ADVANTAGES

Through this method the tracking error can be reduced to zero (excluding transaction costs). Also, full replication is easy to explain and interpret.

### DISADVANTAGES

This method is not practical because of the large number of securities involved and lack of availability of many of these issues. Also, depending on the portfolio size, the weighting accorded each security may be too small to justify a transaction.

## *Optimization Approaches*

The optimization approach uses linear programming (LP) to build an indexed portfolio. An objective function is constructed with the view of optimizing an objective such as maximize yield, maximize convexity, or maximize total return. Appropriate constraints are specified that match the cell breakdown. The linear equation is then solved to give the amounts invested in each cell in order to maximize the objective within the given constraints.

### ADVANTAGES

The optimization approach is systematic and scientific and it can be constructed fairly quickly using a search database and appropriate linear programming software.

### DISADVANTAGES

The results of the approach are dependent on the quality of the database used. The approach is not very flexible, since the portfolio manager does not have the option to rebalance part of the portfolio, if needed.

## *Stratified Sampling or Cell Approach*

In the stratified sampling or cell approach the index is divided into cells, with each cell representing a different characteristic of the index (duration, coupon, maturity, sector, rating, etc.). One or more issues are selected from each cell and invested according to the weight of the cell in the overall index.

Increasing the number of cells in the portfolio will reduce tracking error but will increase the transaction cost. Using too few cells to construct the portfolio will increase the mismatch between portfolio and index, thereby expanding the tracking error.

**ADVANTAGES**

The cell approach gives the portfolio manager some amount of flexibility in constructing the portfolio within the parameters of the cells.

**DISADVANTAGES**

Constructing a fixed income portfolio through stratified sampling is labor-intensive. It is difficult to determine if the portfolio is constructed optimally.

### Variance Minimization Approach

The variance minimization approach uses quadratic programming to estimate a price function that will minimize the variance in the tracking error. In this bond-pricing model, the values of both the portfolio and the index are estimated under different scenarios, in order to obtain the combination of factors that will provide minimum tracking error.

This approach is complex and highly dependent on the data available.

## IO (Interest Only) Obligation

*See* Collateralized Mortgage Obligations.

## Immunization

Immunization is a means of insuring a portfolio against adverse performance, resulting primarily from reinvestment rate risk, through various investment strategies. Following are some of the important strategies in immunization. (*See also* Duration.)

### Cash Flow Matching

Cash flow matching is a method for immunizing a fixed income portfolio from variability of returns by matching cash inflows from the portfolio with cash outflows due on an obligation. This method is also called *dedicating a portfolio*.

Under this method, several bonds are selected to provide the cash flow needed to meet the liabilities due at various points in time. The bonds are selected in such a way that their coupon and principal payments will coincide with the timing of the liabilities.

Using this method, the manager does not have to be concerned about the duration of the portfolio, or rebalancing the portfolio. On the other hand, the process may prove to be more expensive than other immunization methods (such as multiperiod immunization), since the coupon payments may not perfectly match with the liabilities and hence may require additional bonds to cover the liabilities.

This method is typically used in immunizing against pension fund liabilities.

(*See also* Multiperiod Immunization, on the next page.)

### Contingent Immunization

Contingent immunization allows active management of a portfolio while ensuring that the present value of the future obligations will be met. So long as the value of the portfolio of assets remains above the present value of the future obligations, the portfolio is managed actively, because there is a surplus or cushion above the "floor"—that is, the present value of future liabilities. However, once the portfolio value drops to the floor value, active management ceases and the portfolio is immunized, using standard immunization techniques such as duration matching and cash flow matching.

### Dedication Strategy

*See* Cash Flow Matching, above.

### Horizon Matching

Horizon matching is a combination of two immunization strategies—cash flow matching (or dedication) and duration matching (multi-period immunization).

In this strategy the liabilities against which the immunization is being planned are divided into two time periods—a short time period of, say, five years and a longer time period. For the first, shorter time period a cash-matched strategy is used. For the second, longer time period a duration-matched strategy is used to cover the liabilities.

This is a good strategy when nonparallel shifts in the yield curve can affect the value of investments, especially in the short end of the yield curve. The dedicated cash flow matching provides the coverage required during the turbulent days.

### Immunization with Futures

Futures can be used to increase or decrease the duration of a portfolio. The purchase of futures contracts will lengthen the duration, while the sale of futures contracts will shorten it. By increasing or decreasing the duration of the portfolio to match the duration of the liabilities, the fund manager can immunize the portfolio. (*See* Futures Contracts: Section 2.)

### Multiperiod Immunization

Multiperiod immunization is a bond portfolio strategy that ensures that multiple, predetermined liabilities in the future can be met without being affected by interest rate changes. The following conditions are required to achieve immunization:

1. The portfolio duration must be matched against the duration of the liabilities.

2. The distribution of individual asset durations must be greater than the distribution of the duration of the liabilities.

3. The present value of the cash flows from the bond portfolio must be equal to the present value of the future liabilities.

It must, however, be noted that this immunization strategy will work only for nonparallel shifts in the yield curve.

## Mortgage Pass-Through Securities

Mortgage pass-through securities derive their value from an underlying pool of mortgages. These securities give the holder the right to a pro rata share of the cash flows from a pool of mortgage loans.

There are two types of pass-throughs: fully modified pass-throughs and modified pass-throughs.

### Fully Modified Pass-Throughs

Fully modified pass-throughs carry a guarantee from the issuer that the principal and interest payment will be made in a timely manner.

### Modified Pass-Throughs

Modified pass-throughs carry a guarantee of both the interest and principal payments. However, only timely payment of interest is guaranteed. Timely payment of principal is not.

## Nominal Yield

Nominal yield on a bond is the coupon rate. Thus, if a bond pays 12 percent coupon interest, the nominal yield on the bond is 12 percent.

## Noncallable Bonds—Price-Yield Relationship

The price of a noncallable bond can be expressed as the sum of the price of a callable bond and the call premium:

$$P_{NCB} = P_{CB} + C$$

where

$P_{NCB}$ = Price of noncallable bond

$P_{CB}$ = Price of callable bond

$C$ = Call premium

## Option-Adjusted Spread (OAS)

Unlike the *static spread,* the option-adjusted spread (OAS) considers several possible "paths" that future interest rates may take during the life of the bond. These spreads are then used to compute a set of possible values for the bond, from which the market price is determined.

Here are the steps in computing an OAS:

1. Choose an interest rate model with various interest rate "paths."

2. For each "path" calculate the present value of the cash flows using the Treasury rate plus a spread. The result is the path and spread specific (PASS) price.

3. Compute the average PASS price. This is the fair market price for the bond.

OAS measures the extra return that will be earned on a bond with a call feature compared with the return on an equivalent Treasury bond. Thus, OAS overcomes one of the main drawbacks of traditional yield spread analysis—the effect of interest rate volatility and the value of embedded options.

### LIMITATIONS OF OAS

- In an OAS model, OAS is assumed constant throughout the period, whereas in reality OAS is dynamic and can vary over the life of the bond.

- If call value is incorrect, the OAS computed could be wrong.

- The valuation model depends on assumptions about the call and prepayment events. If these assumptions are incorrect, the model will produce unreliable results.

### DIFFERENCE WITH STATIC SPREAD

OAS differs from static spread in that the manager analyzes several possible future paths for interest rates instead of using a single spread to discount all future cash flows.

(*See also* Static Spread.)

## Option-Adjusted Duration (OAD)

Call-adjusted or option-adjusted duration (OAD) is the duration of a callable bond after adjusting for the call option. It can be computed using the formula:

$$OAD = P_{NCB}/P_{CB} \cdot D_{NCB} \cdot (1 - \delta)$$

where

$P_{NCB}$ = Price of noncallable bond

$P_{CB}$ = Price of callable bond

$D_{NCB}$ = Duration of noncallable bond

$\delta$ = Delta of the call option

The option-adjusted duration of a bond depends on three factors:

- The duration of a noncallable bond of the same credit quality.

- The ratio of the price of a noncallable bond and the price of a callable bond of the same credit quality.

- The delta of the bond (ratio of the price of the call option to the price of noncallable bond).

## Option-Adjusted Yield (OAY)

Option-adjusted yield (OAY) is the yield to maturity of a callable bond that is priced by taking into account the call value embedded in the callable bond, such that it equates to an equivalent noncallable bond.

To compute the OAY of a callable bond, first determine the value of the call option embedded in the bond using an option-pricing model. Then calculate the implied value of an equivalent noncallable bond using the following equation:

Price of noncallable bond = Price of callable bond +
   Value of embedded call

The yield to maturity of the callable bond is the option-adjusted yield of the bond, assuming it is priced to equal the implied noncallable bond.

The spread between the option-adjusted yield of a callable bond and the yield to maturity of an equivalent noncallable bond provides an indication of the attractiveness of the callable bond relative to the noncallable bond.

## Pass-Through Certificates

*See* Mortgage Pass-Through Securities.

## Passive Fixed Income Portfolio Strategies

Passive portfolio management strategies are structured to replicate a benchmark with little or no active decision making on the structure of the portfolios or the timing or selection of the securities in the portfolio. A variety of immunization and matching techniques are used to create passive strategies for a fixed income portfolio.

(*See also* Immunization; Cash Flow Matching; Contingent Immunization; Horizon Matching.)

## Pay-in-Kind (PIK) Bonds

Pay-in-kind (PIK) bonds are bonds that give the issuer the option to pay interest in cash or with additional securities. PIKs provide flexibility in managing cash flow.

PIKs are useful when the issuer is not able to support interest payments in cash, but is confident of raising cash eventually through the sale of some illiquid assets (e.g., real estate). Such assets, if forced into sale immediately, may not yield the desired level of cash.

Since these instruments are sold at a premium yield, investors who share the confidence of the issuer may find it attractive.

## PO (Principal Only) Obligations

*See* Collateralized Mortgage Obligations.

## PSA Standard Prepayment Benchmark

The PSA Standard Prepayment Benchmark is a mortgage prepayment standard established by the Public Securities Association (PSA). It is based on the following graduated constant prepayment rate (CPR) for 30-year mortgages.

CPR = 0.2% for the first month, increasing at a rate of 0.2% per month for 30 months

CPR = 6% for months 30 to 360

The above structure is referred to as "100 percent PSA." Specific pools of mortgages may be referred to as having "50 percent PSA" or "150 percent PSA" with reference to the 100 Percent PSA benchmark defined above.

(*See also* Constant Prepayment Rate.)

## Price Value Basis Point (PVBP)

Price value basis point (PVBP) is a measure of bond volatility. It is the change in the price of a bond (in dollars) for one basis point change in the yield.

PVBP is useful in understanding the volatility of a bond. Unlike modified duration, which provides the percentage change in price of a bond, PVBP gives the dollar change in price.

(*See also* Duration; Volatility of Bond Prices.)

## Return on Fixed Income Portfolio

Following are the major factors that influence the return on a fixed income portfolio:

- Changes in the level of interest rates
- Changes in the shape of the yield curve
- Changes in the yield spreads among bond sectors
- Changes in the option-adjusted spreads
- Changes in the yield spread (risk premium) for a particular bond

## Risks, Types and Sources

### Basis Risk

Basis is the spread between the futures price and the spot price. Basis is a key factor in determining prices of many derivatives products. Hence, an unanticipated change in the basis could pose a risk to investors who have used the prevailing basis to price their investments or options. The uncertainty caused by a change in the basis is known as basis risk.

In other words, basis risk is the risk arising out of changes in the spread between the futures price and the spot price.

### Call Risk

A bond may be "called" by the issuer if market interest rates decline below the coupon rate on the bond, since the issuer may find it more economical to refinance the bond.

Investors face three distinct risks as a result of this call provision:

1. Since the issuer will call the bond when market interest rates are declining, the investor faces *reinvestment risk.* When the bond is called, the investor has to reinvest the proceeds at a lower rate.

2. The call provision places a ceiling above which the price of the bond will not appreciate, since the bond will be called away if interest rates decline beyond the coupon rate. This is the *negative convexity* of a callable bond.

3. The possibility of the call being exercised creates *cash flow uncertainty* on the bond.

Investors can cover such a risk by using derivative instruments such as swaps and create a synthetic noncallable bond. (*See* Convexity; Synthetic Noncallable Debt: Section 2.)

### Contraction Risk

Contraction risk in a mortgage-backed security is the risk of an increase in prepayments if interest rates decline. This contracts the expected cash flow, especially for derivatives such as interest-only CMOs. (*See* Collateralized Mortgage Obligations.)

### Credit or Default Risk

Credit or default risk is the risk that issuers of a debt instrument will not be able to honor their commitment with regard to timely payment of interest or principal, or both.

Investors can assess the credit risk of an issuer by using the credit ratings assigned by a commercial rating agency such as Moody's or Standard & Poor's. (*See* Credit Ratings.)

### Event Risk

Event risk relates to any major development—such as the death of a key person in a company or country or the default by a major issuer in the market—that could depreciate the value of an investment.

### Exchange Rate Risk

Exchange rate risk arises from adverse movement in the currency market that depreciates the value of an investment.

Exchange rate risk could be caused by either a decline in the currency of investment or nonavailability of foreign currency to reconvert the investment into the investor's currency.

### Extension Risk

Extension risk in a mortgage-backed security is the possibility of prepayments slowing down as a result of an increase in interest rates. Hence, tranches that were expected to be paid out in a certain period get extended beyond that period.

### Immunization Risk

Immunization strategies work only when the yield curve is flat and when the yield curve shift is parallel. If either of these preconditions does not exist, then the immunized portfolio faces a risk of not being able to meet its immunized objectives.

### Inflation or Purchasing Power Risk

Inflation or purchasing power risk is the risk that the return on an investment will be eroded because of inflation. That is, the real rate of return on the investment becomes zero or negative.

### Interest Rate Risk

Interest rate risk is the risk of decline in value of bond investments because of an unanticipated rise in interest rates.

Interest rate risk consists of two components that work in opposite directions: price risk (or market risk) and reinvestment risk. As interest rates rise, bond prices will fall, but the amount received from reinvestment of coupons will increase because of the increased interest rate. Interest rate risk is normally lower for bonds with higher coupons, and is greater for bonds with longer maturity.

### Liquidity Risk

Liquidity risk is the risk of being unable to liquidate or sell an investment in a reasonable period of time at a reasonable price. Liquidity risk can be identified by the spread between the bid and ask prices. The greater the bid-ask spread, the greater the liquidity risk.

### Political Risk

Political risk is especially important in sovereign credit analysis. It is derived from the following factors:

- The political system of government and the centers of decision making.
- Political tendencies and past political record.
- Stability of political processes and longevity of established processes and mechanisms.
- Integration with international political and financial systems.
- Domestic stability and regional stability.
- Labor relations, demographic distributions, and living standards.

### Prepayment Risk

Prepayment risk is the risk experienced by mortgage-backed securities, arising out of earlier than anticipated prepayments on mortgages. (*See* Contraction Risk; Extension Risk.)

### Reinvestment Risk

When interest rates decline, callable bonds are likely to be called. This leaves the investor with the principal amount, which has to be reinvested at the lower rate. This risk of being compelled to invest at a lower interest rate is called reinvestment risk.

### Sector or Industry Risk

Risk that is specific to an industry sector is known as sector or industry risk. Diversifying investments across different industry sectors can mitigate this risk.

### Yield Curve Risk

Yield curve risk is caused by nonparallel shifts in the yield curve such that interest rates do not change uniformly across the maturity/duration spectrum.

## Rosenberg Propositions

From research findings on international fixed income investing, Michael Rosenberg—author of the seminal article "International Fixed Incoming Investing: Theory and Practice," published in 1995 in *The Handbook of Fixed Income Securities,* 4th ed., Frank J. Fabozzi and T. Dessa Fabozzi, eds., Irwin Professional Publishing—declared that, under a passive investment strategy, creating a currency hedge on a bond portfolio would not produce a significantly different return than an unhedged position. He crystallized this view under two propositions.

### Rosenberg Proposition I

"In the long run, ignoring transaction costs, the amount of risk reduction obtained from international diversification of a bond portfolio is independent of the currency hedge of the portfolio."

### Rosenberg Proposition II

"Taking transaction costs and management fees into consideration, hedged foreign bonds will be a more expensive means of obtaining risk reduction than unhedged foreign bonds."

This proposition is based on the fact that transaction costs and management fees take away as much as 27 to 60 basis points per year. Hence, hedging a passively managed international bond portfolio does not offer any added benefit.

## Samurai Bonds

Samurai bonds are bonds issued in Japan by a foreign country or corporation. For example, a yen-denominated bond issued and sold by IBM-USA in Japan is known as a Samurai bond.

## Serial Bonds

Serial bonds are bonds with a series of maturity dates, each maturity date being a small bond issue by itself.

## Single Monthly Mortality (SMM) Method

*See* Constant Prepayment Rate.

## Sovereign Credit Analysis

Several political factors should be considered in sovereign credit analysis:

- System of government and structures of decision making
- Political tendencies and history
- Longevity of government and process of succession
- Integration with regional trade partners
- Domestic stability
- Labor relations

Economic factors (domestic) should also be taken into consideration:

- Natural resources of the country
- Diversity of industries in the country's economy
- Stability of fiscal and monetary policies
- Levels of inflation and unemployment
- Ease of currency convertibility

Finally, economic factors relating to foreign trade should be accounted for:

- External trade system (trade barriers, NAFTA, etc.)
- Comparison levels of imports vs. exports
- Availability and reliability of sources of foreign exchange
- Foreign currency reserves
- Level of current account deficit
- Foreign investments in domestic projects

There are several key ratios to look at when performing sovereign credit analysis:

- External debt to current account earnings
- Debt service ratio: interest on total debt to current account earnings
- Current account balance to GDP
- Import coverage ratio: net international reserves to one-month imports
- Budget deficit (surplus) to GDP

## Spot Rate

A spot rate is the discount rate used to discount a single future cash flow. The yield to maturity of a zero coupon bond can be termed the spot rate, since it accurately reflects the realizable yield if the bond is held to maturity.

## Springing Issues

Springing issues are bonds whose characteristic may change under certain circumstances. For instance a "poison pill issue" may carry a provision whereby, in the event of a hostile takeover bid on the company, the bonds may be converted into common stock of the company, thus altering the ownership structure of the company, which might thwart the hostile bid.

## Static Spread

Static spread is the spread that will make the present value of the cash flows from a bond, when discounted at the Treasury spot rate plus that spread equal to the current price of the bond. The formula is as follows:

$$P = CF_1/(1 + t_1 + SS) + CF_2/(1 + t_2 + SS) + \ldots$$

where

$P$ = Price of bond

$CF_i$ = Cash flow for period $i$

$t_i$ = Treasury spot rate for period $i$

$SS$ = Static spread

(*See also* Spot Rate.)

## Super Floaters

A super floater is a tranche of a CMO structure with a floating rate, whose coupon rates increase or decrease depending on changes in an underlying index. Super floaters are attractive to investors who believe that market interest rates are expected to rise, since the increased spread under such circumstances will improve the yield.

(*See also* Collateralized Mortgage Obligations.)

## Term Structure of Interest Rates

### Liquidity Preference Hypothesis

According to the liquidity preference hypothesis, rational investors will pay a price premium (demand less yield) for a shorter-term security. In other words, all other things being equal, securities with longer maturities will have a higher yield.

### Loanable Funds Theory

Loanable funds theory holds that interest rates are a function of the supply of and demand for funds.

### Natural Habitat Theory

*See* Segmented Market Theory, below.

### Expectations Hypothesis

According to the expectations hypothesis, the long-term interest rate is the geometric average of the current short-term rate and rates that are expected in the future.

This theory asserts that the shape of the yield curve is primarily determined by the interest rate expectations of investors. It is represented by the formula:

$$(1 + r_2) = (1 + r_1)(1 + {}_1f_1)$$

where

$r_1$ = Current interest rate

$r_2$ = Projected interest rate

${}_1f_1$ = Expected future interest rate

### Segmented Market Theory

Segmented market theory attempts to explain the shape of the yield curve by considering the relative demands for various maturities. This theory claims that borrowers and lenders have preferred "habitats" or are constrained to a specific segment of the yield curve because of their specific requirements.

## Total Return Analysis

The total return on a bond is the current yield plus the average capital gain (loss). It is a more complete measure of return than current yield alone, since it takes into consideration the profit or loss on the investment.

## Tracking Error

Tracking error is caused by the discrepancy between the index return and the indexed portfolio return. It is useful in measuring the performance of a passively managed portfolio, since tracking measures the deviation of returns from a benchmark.

Tracking error is caused by:

- Differences in composition of the portfolio relative to the benchmark.

- Differences in prices used in the benchmark and the portfolio.

- Transaction costs that are incurred by the portfolio (the benchmark assumes no transaction costs).

The objective of an indexed portfolio is to minimize tracking error by managing the above factors.

(*See also* Indexing Strategy).

## Trading Blocs

A trading bloc is a group of international bond markets that are highly correlated.

Five trading blocs can be identified according to their correlation characteristics:

- Dollar bloc (United States, Canada, Australia and New Zealand)

- Core Europe (Germany, France, Netherlands, and Belgium)

- Peripheral Europe (United Kingdom, Denmark, Sweden, Finland, and Portugal)

- Japan

- Emerging markets

Trading blocs are useful in establishing limits on currency exposures, bond positions, liquidity, credit risk, and duration.

Instead of being assigned to individual markets, the limits can be set up for each trading bloc, taking into account the correlations among the markets within each trading bloc.

## Usable Bonds

Usable bonds, sometimes called *synthetic convertibles*, are bonds with warrants attached to them. These warrants give the holder the right to purchase the common stock of the issuer at a specific price.

## Volatility of Bond Prices

The price volatility of a bond is a function of:

- Yield curve behavior
- Coupon rate on the bond
- Remaining term to maturity
- Current price relative to its face value

The longer the maturity of the bond, or the lower its coupon rate, the more volatile the price of that bond is likely to be. Therefore, deep discount bonds and zero coupon bonds experience extreme volatility in price when interest rates change.

Corollary: Short-maturity, high-coupon bonds have lower volatility. These bonds will be preferred when interest rates are rising.

## Yankee Bonds

Yankee bonds are bonds issued in the United States by a foreign country or corporation. For example, a bond issued and sold by a Japanese company in the United States is known as a Yankee bond.

## Yield to Call (YTC)

Yield to call measures the yield that an investor will realize if a callable bond is held until its next immediate call date. YTC provides a more conservative estimate of yield when the bond price is higher or equal to the call price.

An approximate yield to call can be computed by using the formula:

$$YTC = \{CPN + [(CP - MP)/n_c]\}/(CP + MP/2)$$

where

$CPN$ = Coupon on bond

$CP$ = Call price of bond

$MP$ = Market price of bond

$n_c$ = Number of years to call

Like yield to maturity, yield to call is based on some assumptions:

1. The coupon interest received is assumed to be invested at the yield-to-call rate.

2. The bond is assumed to be held until maturity.

3. The bond is assumed to be called on the first call date.

(*See also* Callable Bonds; Yield to Maturity.)


## Yield to Maturity (YTM)

Yield to maturity of a bond is a measure of the average rate of return that will be earned on a bond if held to maturity. It is the single discount rate that equates the present value of the cash flows from a bond to the bond's market price. YTM is also the internal rate of return (IRR) on the bond.

The key assumptions in using YTM include:

1. The cash flows from the interest payments are invested at the computed yield-to-maturity rate.

2. The bond is held to maturity.

The formula for computing yield to maturity is:

Bond price = $CF_1/(1 + r)^1 + CF_2/(1 + r)^2 + \ldots CF_n/(1 + r)^n$

where

$CF_1$ = Cash flow in period $i$

$r$ = Yield to maturity

$n$ = Number of periods

---

### Factoid About Yield to Maturity (YTM)

The YTM of a bond is *higher* than the coupon rate when the bond is trading at a *discount* and *lower* when the bond is trading at a *premium.*

The YTM and current yield will be equal if the coupon rate and market interest rate are equal.

The higher the coupon, the greater the importance of the reinvestment rate assumption.

The longer the maturity, the greater the importance of the reinvestment rate assumption.

---

## Yield to Worst

Yield to worst is the lowest yield from a set of yields calculated for a bond with different call dates.

Assuming that the investor holds the bond throughout the period when different call dates may occur, yield is calculated for each call date. The lowest of these yields is the yield to worst. It is a useful measure that assumes the worst in terms of the timing of the call.

## Z Bond

*See* Collateralized Mortgage Obligations: Z Tranche.

## Zero Volatility Spread

Zero volatility (ZV) spread is the spread that, when added to the discount rate that is used to discount each cash flow, equates the present value of all future cash flows to today's bond price.

Zero volatility spread is useful in analyzing the relative values of securities that have an amortization feature, wherein the principal is paid down periodically, such as mortgage-backed securities.

Following are the steps in computing the ZV spread:

1. Project all cash flows that are likely to occur under different scenarios of prepayments and amortization schedules.

2. Compute the present value of the cash flows under each scenario, using the appropriate Treasury rate with a constant spread as the discount rate.

3. The present value that equates to the bond price today is the appropriate value, and the spread used in computing that present value is the appropriate ZV spread.

The above process will help investors compare and analyze different asset-backed or mortgage-backed securities that have different principal repayment characteristics.

# SECTION 8

# Portfolio Management

## Agency Theory

*See* Agency Friction: Section 1.

## Alpha

Excess return earned over and above the predicted return using an asset-pricing model is known as alpha.

## Arbitrage Pricing Theory (APT)

Arbitrage pricing theory (APT) is an asset-pricing model that uses several factors, based on diversification and arbitrage principles, in determining the price of a security.

$$R_i = E_i + b_{i1}\delta_1 + b_{i2}\delta_2 + \ldots + b_{ik}\delta_k + \epsilon_i \text{ for } i = 1 \text{ to } N$$

where

$R_i$ = Return on asset $i$ during a specified time period

$E_i$ = Expected return on asset $i$

$b_{ik}$ = Reaction in asset $i$'s returns to movements in the common factor

$\delta_k$ = Common factor with a zero mean that influences the returns on all assets

$\epsilon_i$ = Unique effect on asset $i$'s return that, by assumption, is completely diversifiable in large portfolios and has a mean of zero

$N$ = number of assets

Typical factors used in the APT model are:

- Unanticipated change in inflation
- Unanticipated change in industrial production
- Unanticipated change in risk premiums
- Slope of term structure of interest rates

APT is based on three major assumptions:

1. Capital markets are perfectly competitive.
2. Investors always prefer more wealth to less wealth with certainty.
3. The process that generates asset returns can be represented by a factor model.

## Asset Allocation

Asset allocation is the concept of allocating a portfolio of investments across different asset classes with a view to diversifying the risk. Typical asset classes include stocks, bonds, and cash.

Research shows that more than 92 percent of the returns on a portfolio can be attributed to asset allocation decisions. The balance is distributed among market timing, security selection, and other, unexplained factors. Hence, asset allocation is viewed as a very important element in portfolio management.

See Figure 8-1.

## Asset-Backed Securities

Asset-backed securities (ABS) derive their value from the underlying pool of securities, such as mortgage loans or credit

## Figure 8–1  Asset Allocation

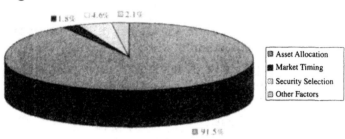

*Nearly 92% of returns result from asset allocation decisions*

card receivables. Popular forms of ABS include collateralized mortgage obligations (CMOs), certificates for automobile receivables (CARs), and mortgage-backed obligations (MBOs).

## Attribution Analysis

Attribution analysis is a framework for decomposing the total return on a portfolio into components such as security selection and market timing. This framework, developed by Brinson and associates in a paper published in 1986, is shown graphically in Figure 8-2.

Using attribution analysis, one can compute the contribution to the total return on investments that is derived from security selection, market timing and other unexplained factors. This way an analyst can determine whether the return on an investment was produced by the investment manager's ability to select the appropriate securities or time the market properly or the return is due to unexplained factors not directly controlled by the manager.

In this figure, passive weights indicate the weight assigned in the benchmark portfolio (such as an index). Active weights are as assigned by the manager. Passive returns are as earned by the benchmark portfolio (index). Active returns are those earned by the actively managed portfolio.

Within the framework, the active market returns can be decomposed as follows:

| Component | Quadrant |
|---|---|
| Market selection | M(II) − M(I) |
| Security selection | M(III) − M(I) |
| Other | M(IV) − M(III) − M(II) + M(I) |
| Total | M(IV) − M(I) |

An extension of this framework can help in global performance attribution analysis by decomposing the returns further into active market returns and active currency returns.

## Figure 8–2   Attribution Analysis Matrix

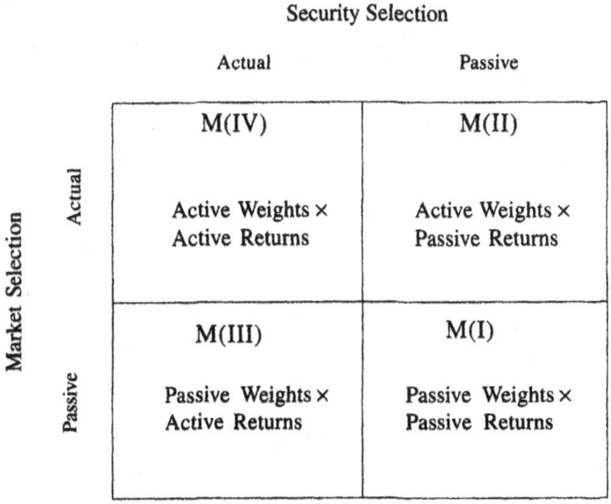

Security Selection

|  | Actual | Passive |
|---|---|---|
| **Actual** | M(IV)<br><br>Active Weights ×<br>Active Returns | M(II)<br><br>Active Weights ×<br>Passive Returns |
| **Passive** | M(III)<br><br>Passive Weights ×<br>Active Returns | M(I)<br><br>Passive Weights ×<br>Passive Returns |

(Market Selection)

## Benchmark

A benchmark is a bogey against which a manager's investment performance can be compared. A good benchmark helps distinguish portfolio performance results that arise from active management skill from those that arise purely from random factors.

The following are characteristics of a good benchmark:

• It should be appropriate to the portfolio being measured. The S&P 500 may be appropriate if you are measuring a large cap fund, but *not* if you are measuring a portfolio predominately invested in small cap companies, since the S&P 500 is populated with large cap companies.

- It should be investible.

- It should be easily measurable.

- It should be identified and specified prior to the evaluation period.

- Its composition should be unambiguous so that the benchmark is easily replicable.

- It should be current, reflecting all available knowledge of the securities in the benchmark.

Here are the steps in constructing or selecting an appropriate benchmark:

1. Identify the key aspects of the manager's investment process.

2. Select securities that are consistent with the manager's investment process.

3. Develop appropriate weights to each security in the benchmark.

4. Review and make appropriate modifications periodically.

5. Rebalance the benchmark portfolio periodically to reflect current trends and changes in the investment process.

### Capital Asset Pricing Model (CAPM)

The capital asset pricing model (CAPM) indicates the expected or required rates of return on risky assets. The formula for determining the price of a security using CAPM is as follows:

$$E(R_i) = RFR + \beta_i(R_m - RFR)$$

where

$E(R_i)$ = Expected return on an investment

$RFR$ = Risk free rate

$\beta_i$ = the beta of the portfolio

$R_m$ = Return on the market portfolio (index)

See Figure 8-3.

CAPM is based on several assumptions:

1. CAPM assumes that investors prefer less risk and more return, which is by and large true. However, recent studies in behavioral finance indicate that investors may be risk seeking in the domain of losses. (*See* Loss Aversion: Section 1.)

2. CAPM assumes that borrowing and lending rates are equal, which clearly is not the case in real markets.

3. CAPM assumes that there are no transaction costs or taxes, which obviously is not valid in the real world.

4. CAPM assumes that betas are stable. Research has shown that they are not and they tend to regress toward the mean over long periods. (*See* Beta: Section 4.)

5. CAPM holds that investors are concerned about nominal, domestic currency returns.

6. CAPM assumes that the market portfolio chosen for comparison is appropriate. Selection of an inappropriate market portfolio is likely to distort the results of CAPM.

## Figure 8–3   Capital Asset Pricing Model

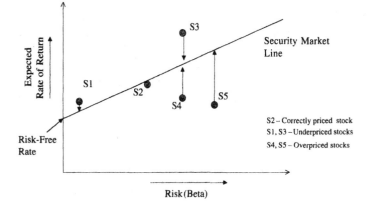

7. CAPM is based on the assumption that investors have homogeneous expectations on risk and return.

For CAPM to hold in an international context, two more assumptions are required:

8. Investors across different markets have identical baskets of goods.

9. Purchase power parity holds.

## Capital Market Line (CML)

The capital market line (CML), shown in Figure 8-4, is the line that links the risk-free rate with the optimal portfolio on an *efficient frontier.* The CML is a key element in the development of the capital asset pricing model (CAPM).

For a summary comparison of performance measures, see Table 8-1 at the end of the section.

(*See also* Capital Asset Pricing Model; Efficient Frontier.)

## Closed-End Fund

A closed-end mutual fund is one that operates like a publicly traded company. Its shares are listed on the stock exchange,

## Figure 8–4    Capital Market Line

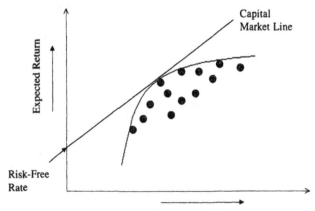

and investors who wish to buy or sell shares in the fund will have to do so in the stock exchange or OTC (over-the-counter) exchanges. Thus, the market price of these shares is determined by supply and demand. The fund itself does not issue more shares, or repurchase the same, once the primary issue is completed.

## Contingent Immunization

*See* Immunization: Section 7.

## Corporate Risk Exposures

A pension plan may be exposed to risks that are similar to the risks faced by the corporate plan sponsor. Plan sponsors must take care to minimize this two-pronged risk.

For instance, a company engaged in biotechnology should avoid investing its pension funds in biotechnology stocks. Otherwise, a downturn in the biotechnology industry, which may affect the company's ability to service its pension obligations, will affect the portfolio at the same time, thus exposing the portfolio to twice the impact of the risk.

(*See also* Surplus Variance.)

## Defined Benefit Plan

*See* Defined Benefit Pension Plan: Section 6.

## Diversification

Diversification is the process by which a portfolio of assets is created such that the unique risk of any single asset is offset by the unique variability of the other assets in the portfolio. This unique risk specific to the asset is also called *unsystematic risk*. After a portfolio is thus diversified, it is left with only undiversifiable risk, also known as *systematic risk*.

A completely diversified portfolio will have a correlation coefficient of +1 with the market portfolio. Studies show that, about 90 percent of the maximum benefit of diversification can be derived from portfolios of 30 to 40 stocks.

See Figure 8-5.
(*See also* Correlation Coefficient: Section 9.)

## Dollar-Weighted Return

*See* Return Computation.

## Dynamic Hedging Strategies

Dynamic hedging strategies can help a portfolio manager continually control the risk on a portfolio of investments by using T-bills or futures in appropriate proportion to the risky assets held in the portfolio. The proportion of funds allocated to the risky asset and the T-bill can be determined using the Black-Scholes pricing model. This proportion is continuously revised to ensure that the combination of risky assets and T-bills (or futures) maintains the desired risk level of the portfolio. As stock (risky asset) prices rise, some T-bills (futures) are sold and the proceeds are used to buy more shares. As stock prices fall, additional shares are sold short and the proceeds are invested in T-bills.

(*See also* Black-Scholes Option Pricing Model; Futures Contracts; Hedging: Section 2.)

## Figure 8–5   Diversification

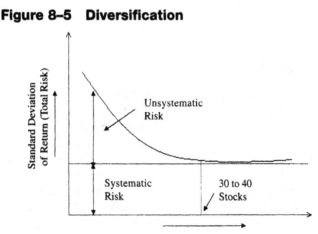

Number of Stocks in Portfolio

## Efficient Frontier

The efficient frontier is the line that represents all possible optimal portfolios in a graph showing the expected returns for given levels of risk.

See Figure 8-6.

(*See also* Modern Portfolio Theory.)

## Implementation Shortfall

Every investment decision is expected to yield a certain return. However, various factors affect the actual return on such an investment. These include the impact cost, timing cost, and opportunity cost of trading. The shortfall between anticipated return from an investment decision and actual return is known as implementation shortfall.

## Indexes

### Dow Jones Industrial Average

The Dow Jones Industrial Average (DJIA) is one of the oldest stock indexes, dating back to 1896. It is a price-weighted index, computed by adding the market prices of the 30 companies in the index and dividing the total by a "divisor." This

## Figure 8–6    Efficient Frontier

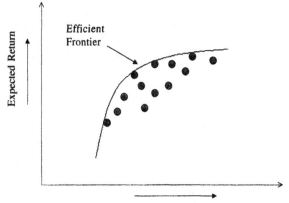

Risk (Standard Deviation of Return)

divisor is used to ensure that stock splits, or addition or deletion of stocks from the index, do not affect the index itself.

The index is made up of 30 blue chip, industrial stocks. The weight of each company in the index is proportional to its share price rather than its market capitalization (share price times number of shares outstanding). Hence, high-priced stocks have a greater impact on the index than low-priced stocks.

The price-weighted Nikkei Average, which is based on 225 stocks of large Japanese companies, is similar to the DJIA.

### S&P 500 Index

The S&P (Standard & Poor's) 500 is a broad index of 500 large cap stocks in the United States. It is weighted by market value, meaning that it compares the total market value of the 500 firms in the index with the total market value of the same firms on the previous day. The percentage increase or decrease in the total market value from one day to the next represents the change in the index. Stock splits do not affect value-weighted indexes.

The S&P 500 Index is included in the U.S. Department of Commerce's leading economic indicators and represents approximately 69 percent of the total value of more than 7200 U.S. stocks. In addition, the 500 stocks in the S&P 500 are divided into nine subsector indexes, covering the financial, technology, utilities, energy, transportation, pharmaceuticals, basic industrials, consumer staples, and consumer services sectors.

Compared with the Dow Jones Industrial Average, the S&P 500 is a more broad-based index and is weighted by market value rather than price. The index is often used as a benchmark to evaluate the performance of equity fund managers.

### Wilshire 5000 Equity Index

The Willshire Index is the most broad-based of the stock indexes, with more than 5000 stocks listed on the New York Stock Exchange (NYSE), American Stock Exchange (AMEX), and NASDAQ in addition to actively traded over-the-counter stocks. The index is based on market value.

## Investment Policy

A written investment policy defines the investment objectives and constraints of the portfolio. It is the document that guides much of the investment decisions on the portfolio.

Specifically, an investment policy should speak to the following elements:

- Risk appetite of the portfolio (client)
- Return requirements
- Liquidity constraints
- Investment time horizon
- Tax considerations
- Legal constraints
- Unique investment circumstances of the portfolio

An investment policy guides the manager on the strategies to be used in achieving investment objectives and provide limits on the types and levels of investments that the portfolio can consider. It also sets the target returns for each asset class in the portfolio and the benchmarks against which performance will be measured.

## Jensen's Alpha

Jensen's alpha measures the excess return earned for a given level of risk. It provides the difference between actual return and required rate of return, as measured by the capital asset pricing model (CAPM).

The formula is as follows:

$$E(R_j) = RFR + \beta_j[E(R_m) - RFR]$$

where

$E(R_j)$ = Expected return on security or portfolio $j$

$RFR$ = Risk-free rate of return for the period

$\beta_j$ = Systematic risk (beta) of security or portfolio $j$

$E(R_m)$ = Expected rate of return on market portfolio

Jensen's alpha measures the value added by a particular investment strategy.

Unlike the Treynor measure or Sharpe ratio, Jensen's alpha requires the use of a different risk-free rate of return for each time interval in the sample period. Like the Treynor measure, Jensen's alpha assumes full diversification of the portfolio as it calculates risk premiums in terms of systematic risk (beta).

For a summary comparison of performance measures, see Table 8-1 at the end of the section.

(*See also* Capital Asset Pricing Model; Sharpe Ratio; Treynor Measure.)

## Load Fund

A mutual fund that charges a fee either up front or at the time of encashment is known as a load fund. Load refers to what the client has to bear, since the fee comes out of the return earned by the client on the investment.

## Market Timing

Market timing is a strategy based on entering and exiting the stock market at specific times when it is appropriate to do so.

Market timing focuses on two techniques:

- Alter asset allocation—for example, by moving into stocks when the market is expected to rise.

- Change risk exposure—for example, by increasing duration if rates are expected to fall.

The effectiveness of market timing can be measured by graphing market movements against portfolio asset allocation or plotting fund returns against market returns. Research has shown that market timing does not work in the long run. If the top 30 trading days were removed, the return would drop from 18 percent to 5 percent.

## Modern Portfolio Theory

Harry Markowitz developed modern portfolio theory in the late 1950s. The foundation of much of modern portfolio management, the theory holds that a single security or portfolio can be identified in the universe of securities or portfolios such that no other security or portfolio of assets offers higher expected return with the same (or lower) risk, or one that has lower risk with the same (or higher) expected return.

Such a security or portfolio lies on what Markowitz termed the *efficient frontier* of securities or portfolios, as shown in Figure 8-7. Markowitz established that it is possible to construct a portfolio of assets, which, for a given level of risk, is the most optimum portfolio as compared with any other portfolio for that given level of risk.

The theory is based on the following assumptions about investor behavior:

1. Investment alternatives are considered according to their probability distribution of expected returns over the holding period.

2. Investors want to maximize their utility in the investment.

3. Investors use the variability of expected returns to estimate the risk of the portfolio.

4. Investment decisions are solely based on the expected risk and return on the investment.

5. Investors prefer higher returns to lower returns and lower risk to higher risk for a given level of return.

### Figure 8–7   Modern Portfolio Theory

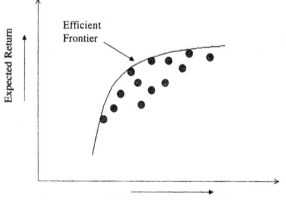

Under these assumptions, an asset or a portfolio of assets is considered efficient if no other asset or portfolio of assets offers higher expected return for a given level of risk, or lower risk for a given level of expected return.

## Net Asset Value (NAV)

Net asset value is a measure that investment companies (mutual funds) use to represent the value of each share in the mutual fund at a given point in time. It is calculated by taking the total market value of the assets (minus the liabilities) of the mutual fund and dividing it by the number of shares outstanding.

Mutual funds in the United States are required to publish their NAVs daily.

## Open-End Fund

Open-end mutual funds continue to sell and repurchase their shares after the initial public offering. These funds are always ready and willing to sell or buy additional shares of the fund at the net asset value (NAV) with or without a charge.

More than 3000 open-end mutual funds, representing over a trillion dollars of assets, are registered in the United States.

## Portfolio Management Strategies

### Buy-and-Hold Strategy

In the buy-and-hold strategy, once a portfolio mix is determined it is held without any change. There is no asset allocation management (hence no management fees), and the portfolio benefits from low turnover and therefore low transaction costs.

The buy-and-hold strategy is appropriate for investors holding a market portfolio. It assumes that investor risk tolerance increases as wealth increases. The strategy produces best results when the long-term trend for a market is upward and the investor holds a market portfolio.

## Constant Mix/Dynamic Rebalancing

The constant mix strategy maintains a constant exposure to all asset classes at all levels of wealth. Whenever asset values change significantly, the portfolio is rebalanced to maintain a constant target mix.

This is a contrarian investing strategy that buys when asset values are falling and sells when asset values are rising. It assumes that the investor's risk tolerance is constant and unvarying. The strategy produces the best results when the markets are volatile and trendless.

## Constant Proportion Portfolio Insurance (CPPI)

CPPI is a strategy based on "portfolio insurance." Implementation follows these steps:

1. Establish a floor limit and invest this amount in risk-free assets.

2. Invest the balance of the assets in high-risk assets in some multiple of the difference between the floor amount and the market value of the portfolio.

3. Purchase (sell) when the value of the high-risk assets increases (decreases).

CPPI is an appropriate strategy for investors whose risk tolerance increases (decreases) with an increase (decrease) in value of the portfolio. It produces optimal results when the market is in a steady and predictable trend.

## Portfolio Rebalancing

A portfolio must be rebalanced when:

- The portfolio has become overpriced, offering potentially inferior future rewards.

- The holdings no longer fit the needs of the client.

- The portfolio is poorly diversified and riskier than it needs to be.

For portfolio managers, rebalancing may be called for when there is a change in the client's needs or circumstances, such as:

- Change in the client's wealth—recognizing, of course, that increased wealth does not automatically mean increased tolerance for risk.

- Change in the client's time horizon—as the time horizon is shortened, the investment mix becomes more conservative.

- Change in liquidity requirements—especially balancing the conflicting requirements of current beneficiaries of the portfolio and the future beneficiaries.

- Change in tax circumstances, laws, and regulations.

- Change in any unique circumstances or preferences of the client.

Availability of new investment alternatives (such as derivatives) that are appropriate to the client's needs may also influence the rebalancing decision. However, a portfolio should not be rebalanced when:

- The chosen investment style is out of favor temporarily.

- The crowd is going in one direction and the investor is going the other way because of a defined strategy or goal.

Investors must recognize that portfolio rebalancing incurs transaction and associated costs. Hence, the value of cost over benefits must be carefully weighed before a portfolio rebalancing decision is made.


## Return Computation

### Dollar-Weighted Return

The dollar-weighted return computes the discount rate that equates a set of periodic cash flows from an investment, when discounted at that rate, to the initial investment. It is also the internal rate of return (IRR) of the investment.

Let's assume that an investor puts $100 into a mutual fund in the first year and $50 in the second year. At the end of the first year the mutual fund pays a dividend of $10. The investor sells the holdings in the mutual fund at the end of the second year at $180. The dollar-weighted return to the investor is computed as follows:

$100 + $50/(1 + r) = 10/(1 + r) + 180/(1 + r)^2$

Inflows                    Outflows

Solving for $r$, we get 15.65 percent, which is the IRR or dollar-weighted return for the investment.

The dollar-weighted rate of return is useful when a manager has some control over the cash inflows and outflows to and from the portfolio.

### Time-Weighted Return

The time-weighted return is the average return on an investment. It is calculated by computing the holding period return for each period under evaluation and then finding the geometric mean of these individual period returns. This method ignores the effect of the cash inflows and outflows to and from the investment during the period.

Let's assume that an investor puts $100 into a mutual fund in the first year and $50 in the second year. At the end of the first year the mutual fund pays a dividend of $10 on the $100. The investor sells the holdings in the mutual fund at the end of the second year at $180. The time-weighted return to the investor is computed as follows:

Return for period 1 = 10%

Return for period 2 = 20%

Geometric average of returns = $\sqrt{(1 + 0.10) \cdot (1 + 0.20)} - 1 = 14.89\%$

A time-weighted rate of return is appropriate when the manager has little or no control over the timing and amount of cash inflows and outflows of the portfolio.

## Security Market Line

The security market line (SML), shown in Figure 8-8, reflects the combination of risk and return on various risky assets available in the capital market at a given time.

The SML can change in three different ways:

1. Individual investments or asset classes may change position on the SML as their perceived risk changes.

# Figure 8–8    Security Market Line

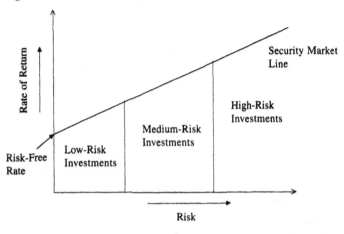

2. The overall slope of the SML may change because of a change in the investor's attitude toward risk.

3. The SML may shift in a parallel fashion because of a change in the real risk-free rate or the expected rate of inflation.

The SML is useful for understanding the relative risk-return characteristics of various instruments and asset classes. (*See also* Capital Asset Pricing Model.)

## Sharpe Ratio

The Sharpe ratio measures the amount of excess return earned for every unit of additional total risk taken by the portfolio. It is expressed by the formula:

$$S_i = (R_i - RFR)/SD_i$$

where

$S_i$ = Sharpe ratio for portfolio $i$

$R_i$ = Average rate of return on portfolio $i$ for a specific period

$RFR$ = Risk-free rate of return during the time period

$SD_i$ = Standard deviation of the rate of return for portfolio $i$ during the time period.

The Sharpe ratio is useful for measuring the performance of a portfolio that contains both systematic and unsystematic risk (i.e., not fully diversified).

The Sharpe ratio is often used in conjunction with the Treynor measure. For a fully diversified portfolio, the two measures will give identical results. However, a poorly diversified portfolio will receive a high ranking under the Treynor measure but a low ranking under the Sharpe ratio.

For a summary comparison of performance measures, see Table 8-1 at the end of the section.

(*See also* Treynor Measure.)

## Strategic Asset Allocation

Strategic asset allocation is the long-run, secular allocation of a portfolio across different asset classes. This allocation is largely based on the long-run, average level of risk tolerance of the investor as well as the long-run, past performance and future expectation of the asset classes.

## Surplus Variance

Surplus variance is the potential variance, over time, of the difference between the value of a pension plan's assets and value of its liabilities. Plan sponsors are typically concerned about this risk in addition to other normal investment risks.

## Systematic and Unsystematic Risk

Systematic risk is the risk that cannot be reduced through diversification. It is also called the *market risk,* since anyone invested in the market will have to bear it.

Unsystematic risk is the risk that can be eliminated through diversification. This risk is specific to a stock or industry sector to which the stock belongs. The factors that have a negative effect on one specific industry can have a positive influence on another industry. Hence, a diversified portfolio that has exposure to both industries limits the risk specific to each of the industries and stocks.

## Tactical Asset Allocation

Tactical asset allocation helps investors take advantage of perceived inefficiencies in the relative prices of securities in different asset classes. Tactical asset allocation is based on expected returns, as well as the risks of and correlations among various asset classes. It typically does not consider changes in the investor's risk tolerance.

## Time-Weighted Return

*See* Return Computation.

## Trading Costs

### Impact Cost

Impact cost (or market impact) is the change in price between the time an order is placed with a broker and the time it is executed by the broker. It is also called the *intraday cost,* or the cost of buying liquidity.

See Figure 8-9.

### Timing Cost

Timing cost is the change in price between the time the order is received by a broker and the time it is presented to the market. Also called the *interday cost,* it is the cost of not executing the total order at once out of fear that the market will move.

See Figure 8-9.

### Opportunity Cost

Opportunity cost is the change in price between the time an order is placed and the time it is canceled. It is the cost of liquidity failure, incurred by not executing the trade.

Research shows that transaction costs are higher for momentum managers than for value managers.[1] Since momen-

---

[1]Wayne H. Wagner, "Defining and Measuring Trading Costs Execution Techniques," in *Trading Costs and the Microstructure of Markets* (AIMR, 1993).

## Figure 8–9   Timing Cost vs. Impact Cost

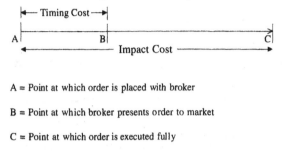

A = Point at which order is placed with broker

B = Point at which broker presents order to market

C = Point at which order is executed fully

tum managers are buyers of liquidity, they base their decisions on news or earnings. Hence, prices tend to rise even while their decisions are made and while the orders are executed. On the other hand, value managers tend to be liquidity suppliers to the market. Hence, they are able to keep the transaction costs low.

Transaction costs of passive managers tend to be higher than those for value managers but lower than those for momentum managers, since passive decisions are not triggered by an excess supply or on momentum.

### Treynor Measure

Treynor's measure indicates a portfolio's excess return per unit of risk. It is represented by the formula:

$$T = (R_i - RFR)/\beta_i$$

where

$R_i$ = Average rate of return for portfolio $i$ during a specified time period

$RFR$ = Average rate of return on a risk-free investment during the time period

$\beta_i$ = Slope of the portfolio's characteristic line during the time period (i.e., the portfolio's relative volatility)

The Treynor measure is useful for evaluating a completely diversified portfolio, since it implicitly assumes that systematic risk is the relevant risk measure, and that unsystematic risk has been diversified away.

For a summary comparison of performance measures, see Table 8-1.

(*See also* Sharpe Ratio.)

## Table 8-1   Summary Comparison of Performance Measures

| Sharpe Ratio | Alpha of CML | Treynor's Measure | Jensen's Alpha |
|---|---|---|---|
| **FORMULA** | | | |
| $(r_p - r_f)/\sigma_p$ | $r_a - \{r_f + [(r_m - r_f)/ \sigma_m]\sigma_A\}$ | $(r_p - r_f)/\beta_p$ | $r_a - [r_f + (r_m - r_f)\beta_a]$ |
| where | where | where | where |
| $r_p$ = Return on portfolio | $r_a$ = Return on asset | $r_p$ = Return on portfolio | $r_a$ = Return on asset |
| $r_f$ = Risk-free rate of return | $r_f$ = Risk-free rate of return | $r_f$ = Risk-free rate of return | $r_f$ = Risk-free rate of return |
| $\sigma_p$ = Standard deviation of portfolio (representing total risk) | $r_m$ = Return on market portfolio | $\beta_p$ = Beta of portfolio | $r_m$ = Return on market portfolio |
| | $\sigma_m$ = Standard deviation of market portfolio | | $\beta_a$ = Beta of asset |
| | $\sigma_A$ = Standard deviation of asset | | |
| **MEASUREMENT VALUES** | | | |
| Gives slope of capital market line (CML). | Indicates relative distance from CML. | Gives $\beta$ from capital asset pricing model (CAPM). | Indicates relative distance from CML. |
| Measures excess return per unit of risk (total risk). | Measures excess return for a given level of risk (total risk). | Measures excess return per unit of systematic risk. | Measures excess return for a given level of systematic risk. |
| Used to evaluate a portfolio representing majority of the total investments. | Used to assess additional return earned for the given level of risk. | Used to evaluate part of a portfolio or specific asset. | Measures value added by a strategy. |
| Uses total risk as the risk measure. | Uses total risk as the risk measure. | Uses $\beta$ (systematic risk) as the risk measure. | Uses $\beta$ (systematic risk) as the risk measure. |

# SECTION 9

# Quantitative Techniques

## Autocorrelation

Autocorrelation in a multiple regression indicates that the residuals (the difference between actual and predicted value) are correlated among themselves.

Omission of an important explanatory variable and incorrect definition of the relationship between the variables are two main reasons for autocorrelation.

Positive autocorrelation leads to underestimation of the standard error of the estimated coefficients. This will result in a high T statistic, leading to the erroneous conclusion that the coefficients are significant when in fact they are not.

(*See also* Standard Error; T Statistic.)

## Correlation

*See* Correlation Coefficient.

## Correlation Coefficient

The correlation coefficient measures the degree of association between two variables. This relationship could be positive (positive correlation) or negative (negative correlation).

The correlation coefficient is always between −1 and +1: −1 indicates perfect negative correlation and +1 indicates perfect positive correlation.

The coefficient is useful in determining how a particular stock is correlated with the market and how two stocks are correlated with each other. The information is helpful in guiding decisions on diversification of a portfolio.

For example, when a stock has a correlation of +0.8 with the stock market, it is highly, positively correlated with the market. That is, the stock's performance is closely linked to the performance of the market. The correlation of a stock with a stock market is also known as *beta*.

Estimating the correlation between two stocks requires the following information:

- Standard deviation of stock A
- Standard deviation of stock B
- Covariance between stock A and stock B

The formula for computing the correlation coefficient between two stocks is:

$$R_{AB} = (COV_{AB})/ \sigma_A \sigma_B$$

where

$R_{AB}$ = Correlation coefficient

$COV_{AB}$ = Covariance between stock A and stock B

$\sigma_A$ = Standard deviation of stock A

$\sigma_B$ = Standard deviation of stock B

(*See also* Beta: Section 4; Covariance; Standard Deviation.)

## Coefficient of Determination

The coefficient of determination measures the extent to which the variation in the dependent variable is explained by the regression equation.

(*See also* $R^2$.)

## Covariance

Covariance measures the extent to which the returns on two risky assets move in tandem.

A positive covariance means that the returns of the two assets move together. A negative covariance means that the returns vary inversely. The formula is given by:

Covariance of $i$ and $j = \sum (i - m_i)(j - m_j)/n$

where

$i$ = Prices of stock $i$

$m_i$ = Mean value of prices of stock $i$

$j$ = Prices of stock $j$

$m_j$ = Mean value of prices of stock $j$

$n$ = Number of prices used in the computation

Covariance is an absolute measure of the extent to which two sets of numbers move together over time, as compared with the correlation coefficient, which is a relative measure.

(*See also* Correlation Coefficient.)

## Discounting

Discounting is the process by which the present value of a future cash flow is computed. A discount rate is the rate that discounts the future cash flow to its present value.

(*See also* Present Value.)

## Dummy Variables

Dummy variables are used in regression analysis to eliminate some definition errors or variance errors such as heteroskedasticity. Such variables usually take on values of 0 or 1.

(*See also* Heteroskedasticity.)

## Durbin-Watson Test

The Durbin-Watson Test provides a measure of the autocorrelation between different variables in a multiple regression model. A Durbin-Watson number between 1.45 and 2.55 indicates that *no* autocorrelation is present among the variables.

(*See also* Autocorrelation.)

## F Statistic

The F statistic is a measure of the explanatory power of the regression taken as a whole. It indicates the statistical significance of all the independent variables combined.

For example, an F ratio of 5.33 is significant for a regression equation, since the F statistic (derived from a standard F-statistic table) is 3.19 at 5 percent level of significance with degrees of freedom (2,47). Degrees of freedom indicates the number of independent pieces of data available for computing variability of a set of data.

A high F statistic (greater than the number derived from a standard F-statistic table) indicates that the regression as a whole is significant. That is, there is a strong relationship between the dependent variable and all the independent variables combined.

## Future Value

Future value is the amount of money an investment will grow to over a given period of time at a given interest rate.

The formula for computing the future value of an investment is:

$$FV = PV \cdot (1 + r)^n$$

where

$FV$ = Future value of investment

$PV$ = Present value of investment

$r$ = Rate of interest per period

$i$ = Number of periods

Note that if an investment is compounded every quarter, the interest rate ($i$) must be for the quarter, and the number of periods ($n$) will be 4 for the year.

## Heteroskedasticity

Heteroskedasticity occurs when the variance between actual and predicted value is not constant across all observations. The problem can be corrected by using a dummy variable.

## Hypothesis Testing

Hypothesis testing is a method by of determining whether a statistical result from a sample data set is significant—that is, whether the result can be applied to the entire population.

## Kurtosis

Kurtosis measures the fatness of the tails of a probability distribution. A large kurtosis indicates that a large number of observations lie well beyond the mean.

## Least Squares Method

The least squares method identifies the line that best explains a relationship between two variables. This is the regression line that has the lowest value for the sum of the squares of the errors. Hence, it is termed the *least squares regression*.

## Lower Partial Moments (LPM)

Lower partial moments measure the uncertainty of falling below target outcome level. LPM is useful in measuring the riskiness of an investment when only the downside potential is of concern.

## Multi-colinearity

Multi-colinearity occurs in a regression model when two or more independent variables are not independent of each other, but are correlated.

High correlation coefficients between the variables of the regression equation may indicate the presence of multi-colinearity. For example, a high F statistic, combined with a low T statistic indicates multi-colinearity. Multi-colinearity can be avoided by dropping a variable before performing the regression and/or by increasing the sample size.

## Multiple-Regression Analysis

Multiple-regression analysis examines the relationship between one variable and two or more variables, as compared with simple regression, which analyses the relationship between two variables.

## Present Value

Present value is the current value of a future cash flow. It is computed by discounting the future cash flow at the appropriate discount rate. The formula is as follows:

$$PV = FV / (1 + r)^n$$

where

$PV$ = Present value

$FV$ = Future value (or future cash flow expected)

$r$ = Discount rate per period

$n$ = Number of periods in the future when the cash flow will occur

(*See also* Discounting; Future Value.)

## $R^2$

The $R^2$ of a simple two-factor regression model measures how much of the variability of one factor is explained by the variability of the other factor. A regression equation with a high $R^2$ indicates high reliability of the results of the regression analysis.

## Regression Analysis

Regression analysis helps the analyst determine the nature of the relationship between two or more variables from empirical observations. In order to perform regression analysis, the analyst must identify the dependent variable and the independent variable(s) and then determine a mathematical equation that represents the relationship between these variables.

(*See also* Least Squares Method.)

## Statistical Measures

### Arithmetic Mean

The arithmetic mean is the most common average of a set of numbers. It is computed using the formula:

$$AM = (a_1 + b_2 + c_3 \ldots + m_n)/n$$

where

$a, b, c$ = Set of numbers

$m_n$ = The last number in the series

$n$ = Number of items comprising the set

For example, in the series $1, 2, 4, 6, 6, 8, 12$, the mean is 5.57.

### Geometric Mean

The geometric mean is useful in computing the average return on an investment over a period of time. It is computed using the formula:

$$GM = \{(1 + r_1)(1 + r_2) \ldots (1 + r_n)\}^{(1/n)} - 1$$

where $r_1 \ldots r_n$ is a set of returns and $n$ is the total number.

For example, for the set of returns $14\%, 12\%, 8\%, 15\%$:

$$GM = \{(1.14)(1.12)(1.08)(1.15)\}^{(1/4)} - 1 = 12.22\%$$

### Median

The median is the value of the middle number in a series, arranged in ascending order. If the series has an even number of values, then the median is the average of the two values located in the middle.

For example, in the series $1, 2, 4, 6, 8, 10, 12, 14$, the median is the average of the fourth-place and fifth-place numbers, or $(6 + 8)/2 = 7$.

## Mode

The mode is the number that occurs in a series most frequently.

For example, in the series 1, 2, 4, 6, 6, 8, 12, the mode is 6, which occurs twice.

---

### Factoid About Statistical Measures

The geometric mean is always less than the arithmetic mean unless the numbers are equal.

The difference between the arithmetic mean and geometric mean increases as the variation of the numbers increases.

The mean, median, and mode are equal if the sample is normally distributed.

---

## Skewness

Skewness measures the extent of variation from the symmetrical, normal distribution pattern.

The measure of skewness is the third moment, or $M_3$. It is measured as the average of the cubes of the differences between each value of a variable and its mean. (The mean is the first moment, $M_1$, and the variance is the second Moment, $M_2$.)

A positively skewed distribution pattern has a longer tail to the right of the mean. A negatively skewed distribution has a longer tail to the left of the mean.

Skewness is represented by the formula:

$$M_3 = \sum (x - \mu)^3 / N$$

where

$M_3$ = Skewness

$x$ = The number in the series

$\mu$ = The mean of the series

$N$ = The total numbers in the series

## Standard Deviation

The standard deviation is used as a measure of absolute (unsystematic) risk. It is the square root of variance.

Standard deviation of $\sigma = \sqrt{\sigma_x^2}$

where $x$ is the value of the variable and $\sigma_x^2$ is the variance.

In a normal distribution 68 percent of the sample observations typically fall within one standard deviation; 95 percent fall within two standard deviations and 98 percent fall within three standard deviations.

The standard deviation is useful as a measure of the unsystematic risk for various types of investment securities. However, it has some significant limitations:

1. The standard deviation is useful only in measuring symmetrical patterns of distribution, where the upside risks equal the downside risks. However, it is unable to accommodate an asymmetric payoff profile, such as that of options and portfolio insurance strategies. Thus, the standard deviation is limited to those asset classes whose returns follow a normal distribution.

2. Because of its statistical nature, the standard deviation is unable to reflect behavioral aspects of investing.

3. The standard deviation ignores the mean return as a reflection of the risk of an investment.

4. The standard deviation is based on a probability distribution curve. Since returns on assets are not stable over time, the standard deviation must be computed anew for different time periods.

(*See also* Systematic and Unsystematic Risk: Section 8; Variance.)


## Standard Error

The standard error estimates the degree to which a regression equation does not fit the data plotted.

It is calculated by comparing the squared differences between (1) the actual values of the dependent variable ($y$) for each value of the independent variable ($x$) and (2) the theoretical value of the dependent variable ($y'$) as given by the regression equation.

The standard error helps determine the accuracy of the regression equation against the actual plot.

## T Statistic

The T statistic is a measure of the explanatory power of the coefficient of a single independent variable in a regression equation. It indicates whether an individual coefficient is significant. The formula is as follows:

T statistic = Value of coefficient/Standard error

In a normally distributed set of data, at the .01 significance level (or 99 percent confidence level) a T statistic above 2.66 is considered significant.

## Type I and II Errors

Before a hypothesis can be implemented, it must be tested for significance. Hypothesis testing determines whether the hypothesis is true or false.

- Rejecting a hypothesis when it is actually true is a *Type I error.*

- Accepting a hypothesis when it is actually false is a *Type II error.*

## Variance

Variance measures the dispersion of a random variable from its mean. Specifically, it is a measure of the average squared difference of each value of the variable from the mean:

Variance $\sigma_x^2 = \sum (x - \mu)^2 / N$

where

$x$ = Value of variable

$\mu$ = Mean value of variable

$N$ = Number of occurrences of variable

The higher the value of the variance, the greater the dispersion of the variable. Variance is another measure of the absolute risk of a portfolio.

(*See also* Modern Portfolio Theory: Section 8.)

# SECTION 10

# Real Estate Investments

## Bottom-up Approach

The bottom-up approach to real estate investments emphasizes asset-by-asset selection of properties. Through this approach an investor seeks to identify individual mispriced properties.

## Commingled Real Estate Funds (CREFs)

Commingled real estate Funds (CREFs) are similar to REITs but differ in their performance and other factors, as described in Table 10-1.

(*See also* Real Estate Investment Trusts.)

## Real Estate Investment Trusts (REITs)

A real estate investment trust is a structure that provides investors with exposure to the real estate market without

## Table 10-1   CREFs vs. Real Estate Investment Trusts (REITs)

|                                        | CREF                                           | REIT                                                  |
| -------------------------------------- | ---------------------------------------------- | ----------------------------------------------------- |
| Historical returns                     | Mediocre                                       | Very good                                             |
| Basis for asset pricing                | Appraisal-based                                | Transaction-based                                     |
| Inflation hedge                        | Good                                           | Not good                                              |
| Diversification: correlation with stocks | Correlation with equity low, but not low enough | More like equity; hence correlation with equity high  |
| Liquidity                              | Very low                                       | Very good                                             |
| Leverage                               | Unlevered                                      | Levered                                               |
| Inflation hedge                        | Good                                           | Poor                                                  |
| Returns calculation                    | Returns after fees                             | Returns before fees                                   |

Source: David H. Downs and David J. Hartzell, "Real Estate Investment Trusts," in *The Handbook of Real Estate Portfolio Management,* Joseph I. Paglian Jr., ed. (Irwin, 1995).

direct exposures to specific properties. REIT shares trade on organized exchanges, just as stocks do, and provide investors with a pro rata interest in a pool of real estate properties.

REITs provide several advantages to the investor:

1. REITs offer an effective means of diversifying a real estate portfolio without a large capital outlay.

2. REITs are fairly liquid, since they trade on exchanges, like stocks.

3. REITs allow smaller funds to participate in real estate without a large commitment of research and analysts.

4. Unique real estate investment skills are not needed to gain exposure to real estate through REITs.

On the other hand, REITs have a high correlation with small cap stocks; hence, they provide less diversification benefits with respect to small cap stocks.

See Table 10-1 for a comparison of REITs and commingled real estate funds (CREFs).

## Real Estate Mortgage Investment Conduit (REMIC)

A real estate mortgage investment conduit (REMIC) is a type of collateralized mortgage obligation (CMO) that converts a CMO from a debt instrument to an equity-type investment. A share in a REMIC represents a proportionate interest in a pool of real estate investments, similar to a REIT.

REMICs offer the issuing bank the advantage of removing the debt from its balance sheet.

(*See also* Collateralized Mortgage Obligations: Section 7.)

## Real Estate Values

Seven factors affect the value of real estate investments:

- Interest rates
- Legislation/tax changes
- Economic conditions
- Vacancy rates/supply conditions
- Demographic trends
- Location
- Condition of property

## Risk Factors of Real Estate Investments

### Systematic Risk

Systematic risk is the nondiversifiable risk carried by the national real estate market. It is affected by factors such as federal taxation policies, inflation, cap rates (risk premiums), discount rates, the business cycle, and the term structure of interest rates.

### Unsystematic Risk

Unsystematic risk is the diversifiable risk applicable to the regional market.

Diversifiable factors that affect unsystematic risk include demographic trends in the region, income growth of the population, and vacancies and growth in the region's employment base. An example of a regional, diversifiable factor is heavy concentration of software-related jobs in one area or region. If the software industry suffers a recession, the real estate property values in this region will be uniformly and adversely affected.

- Diversifiable factors that affect the local market include construction costs, state and local taxes, income levels, and vacancy rates.

- Property-specific risks that can be diversified away include location of the property, lease structure, financing, property age, property condition, and quality of property management.

## Top-Down Approach

Under the top-down approach to real estate investments, an investor evaluates the national real estate market, selects regional market(s), identifies the local market, and then makes a specific property selection.

This approach is useful in diversifying real estate investments.

## Valuation Methods

### Cost Method

The cost method of real estate valuation is based on the market value of the land on which the property is situated and the depreciated value of the building and any improvements. The method is usually used to value relatively new properties whose cost and market value do not differ substantially.

The cost method may not give an accurate reflection of the value of a real estate property, since land values are not readily comparable if similar properties are rarely sold. Also, the depreciated amount of the structure on the property could be a subjective estimate.

### Sales Comparison Method

The sales comparison method is based on an evaluation of transactions of similar properties in the recent past.

The method employs a gross income multiplier (GIM) to determine the market value of the property. For each comparable property, the GIM is computed by the following formula:

GIM = Sale price/Gross annual income

An average of the various GIMs applied to the gross annual income from the property leads to an estimate of fair market value:

Estimated market value of property = Average GIM ·
Gross annual income from property

Since most real estate properties are unique, this method is not entirely reliable. Also, some properties may be sold at distress prices for various reasons. Hence, the prices may not be entirely comparable. Thus, the sales comparison method is not appropriate for evaluating complex properties with unique characteristics, such as shopping malls and office complexes.

## Income Method

The income method uses the discounted cash flow (DCF) model to assess the value of a real estate property in terms of its capacity to generate future cash flow. The method relies on the "direct income capitalization" approach to determine income-generating value according to the formula:

Market value = $NOI/(r - g)$

where

$NOI$ = Net operating income

$r$ = Required rate of return

$g$ = Estimated growth rate of $NOI$

The income method is considered fairly objective. However, since estimates of future rent levels are based on forecasts of economic conditions, a subjective element enters into the computation.

(For a description of the DCF model, *see* Company Valuation Models: Section 6.)

## Articles and Papers

"Behavioral Risk: Anecdotes and Disturbing Evidence," Arnold S. Wood, in *Investory Worldwide VI* (AIMR, 1996).

"Benchmark Portfolios and the Manager/Plan Sponsor Relationship," Jeffrey V. Bailey, Thomas M. Richards, and David E. Tierney, in *Current Topics in Investment Management,* Frank J. Fabozzi and T. Dessa Fabozzi, eds. (HarperCollins, 1990).

"Constructing Fixed Income Portfolios," Chris P. Dialynas, in *Improving the Investment Decision Process—Better Use of Economic Inputs in Securities Analysis and Portfolio Management* (AIMR, 1992).

"Defining and Measuring Trading Costs," Wayne H. Wagner, in *Execution Techniques, True Trading Costs, and the Microstructure of Markets* (AIMR, 1993).

"Disentangling Equity Return Regularities," Bruce I. Jacobs and Kenneth N. Levy, in *Equity Markets and Valuation Methods* (AIMR, 1988).

"Dynamic Strategies for Asset Allocation," Andre F. Perold and William F. Sharpe, in *Financial Analysts Journal,* (AIMR, January–February 1988).

"The Effects of Budget Deficit Reduction on the Exchange Rate," Craig S. Hakkio, in *Economic Review,* Federal Reserve Bank of Kansas City (Third Quarter, 1996).

"Engineered Investment Strategies: Problems and Solutions," Robert L. Hagin, in *Equity Markets and Valuation Methods* (AIMR, 1988).

"Guide to Evaluating Sovereign Credits," Aida Der Hovanesian, in *Fixed Income Credit Research,* Morgan Stanley & Co. (November 1992).

"International Bond Portfolio Management," Christopher B. Steward and J. Hank Lynch, Ch. 26 in *Managing Fixed Income Portfolios,* Frank J. Fabozzi, ed. (Frank J. Fabozzi Associates, 1997).

"International Fixed Income Investing: Theory and Practice," Michael R. Rosenberg, Ch. 49 in *The Handbook of Fixed Income Securities,* 4th ed. Frank J. Fabozzi and T. Dessa Fabozzi, eds. (Irwin, 1995).

"Myopic Loss Aversion and the Equity Premium Puzzle," Shlomo Benartzi and Richard H. Thaler, in *Quarterly Journal of Economics,* MIT Press (February 1995).

"The Nature of Effective Forecasts," David B. Bostian Jr., in *Improving the Investment Decision Process—Better Use of Economic Inputs in Securities Analysis and Portfolio Management* (AIMR, 1992).

"Option-Adjusted Spread Analysis: Going Down the Wrong Path?" Robert W. Kopprasch, in *Financial Analysts Journal,* AIMR (May–June, 1994).

"The Psychology of Risk," Amos Tversky, in *Quantifying the Market Risk Premium Phenomenon for Investment Decision Making* (AIMR, 1990).

"Real Estate Investment Trusts," David H. Downs and David J. Hartzell, Ch. 14 in *The Handbook of Real Estate Portfolio Management,* Joseph I. Pagliari Jr., ed. (Irwin, 1995).

"The Use of Futures in Immunized Portfolios," Jes B. Yawitz and William J. Marshall, *Journal of Portfolio Management* (Institutional Investor, Winter 1985).

"Value at Risk—New Approaches to Risk Management," Katerina Simons, in *New England Economic Review,* Federal Reserve Bank of Boston (September–October 1996).

## Books

*The Analysis and Use of Financial Statements,* Gerald I. White, Ashwinpaul C. Sondhi, and Dov Fried (John Wiley & Sons, 1994).

*Analysis for Financial Management,* 4th ed., Robert C. Higgins (Irwin Professional Publishing, 1995).

*Applied Regression: An Introduction,* Michael S. Lewis-Beck (Sage Publications, 1980).

*Bond Markets: Analysis and Strategies,* 3d ed., Frank J. Fabozzi (Prentice-Hall, 1996).

*Competitive Advantage: Creating and Sustaining Superior Performance,* Michael E. Porter (The Free Press, 1985).

*Economics: Private and Public Choice,* 7th ed., James D. Gwartney and Richard L. Stroup (Dryden Press, 1995).

*Fundamentals of Corporate Finance,* 2d ed., Stephen A. Ross, Randolph W. Westerfield, and Bradford D. Jordan (Irwin Professional Publishing, 1993).

*Futures, Options, and Swaps,* 2d ed., Robert W. Kolb (Blackwell, 1997).

*Global Asset Management and Performance Attribution,* Dennis S. Karnosky and Brian D. Singer (ICFA Research Foundation, 1994).

*The Handbook of Fixed Income Securities,* 4th ed., Frank J. Fabozzi and T. Dessa Fabozzi (Irwin Professional Publishing, 1995).

*Investment Analysis and Portfolio Management,* 4th ed., Frank K. Reilly (Dryden, 1994).

*Investments,* 2d ed., Zvi Bodie, Alex Kane, and Alan J. Marcus (Irwin Professional Publishing, 1993).

*Managing Investment Portfolios: A Dynamic Process,* 2d ed., John L. Maginn and Donald L. Tuttle (Warren, Gorham & Lamont, 1990).

*Standards of Practice Handbook,* 7th ed. (AIMR, 1996).

*Understanding Regression Analysis: An Introductory Guide,* Larry D. Schroeder, David L. Sjoquist, and Paula E. Stephan (Sage Publications, 1986).